I love this book! It is not just a "how-to" book--it is a collection of fascinating stories as the Holy Spirit taught Mike how to partner with Him. And in reading those stories, we learn how to do the same.

I think it should be required reading for anyone in ministry. As Mike points out, however, we are all in ministry, and few books are like this in the way it teaches us how to minister where we are. That can transform entire segments of society which, perhaps, no one except us is in a position to do.

Mike demonstrates not only how to move in God's power, but how to reflect His heart, whose beauty can melt the hardest of defenses and transform lives. That very heart comes through in this book which will transform all who read it into a people filled with faith and the realization that we can bring God's presence into any situation--wherever He has placed us in this life.

Randy Fisk
Author of "The Presence, Power and Heart of God"

Mike Smith is a Follower of Jesus who shares with the reader a genuine invitation to discover living the life of the Kingdom of God. With his honest writing and discovery, Mike's story welcomes us to learning to live like Jesus. A daily life where God is busy moving in the lives of the people all around us. While at the same time inviting us to partner with that work of reconciling people to God. Perhaps what I have loved most in reading Mike's story, is that He is a sincere person learning to follow Jesus in the power of the Holy Spirit. He shares how God's love has filled his heart for the people of his workplace and community.

You will discover in this book a fresh invitation to a dynamic life of following Jesus and bringing his kingdom into the earth, right where we live each day, even as it is in heaven. This book is the story of a real person, with a real faith in a real and living God. I loved reading Mike's book and appreciated the activations that he has included to help us engage in next steps of daily discipleship.

Kirk Delaney
Senior Pastor - Pine Rivers Vineyard Church
National Director - Vineyard Churches Australia

Michael Smith is one of those few people who has true passion for God. When Mike talks about God, he radiates and the person he is talking to knows that he/she is talking to someone who knows Jesus personally. Mike is always willing and ready to pray and help other people. I am very happy that Mike wrote this book because he is a very honest man and through the stories of his life he allows us to discover the never ending Love of Jesus and His real Presence in the current world.

Dariusz Jadusinski
Entrepreneur/Catholic Charismatic Community Leader

LEAP

LEAP

TRANSFORMING YOUR WORKPLACE FOR JESUS

MICHAEL D SMITH

PUBLISHED BY
MICHAEL D SMITH
ALLEN, TX

© 2021, Michael D Smith

All rights reserved. No part of this document may be reproduced or transmitted in any form or by any means, electronic, mechanical, photocopying, recording, or otherwise, without prior written permission of the publisher.

Paperback   ISBN: 978-1-7370440-0-0
Digital   ISBN: 978-1-7370440-1-7 (epub version)

Library of Congress Control Number: 2021907890

Scriptures marked NLT are taken from the HOLY BIBLE, NEW LIVING TRANSLATION (NLT): Scriptures taken from the HOLY BIBLE, NEW LIVING TRANSLATION, Copyright© 1996, 2004, 2007 by Tyndale House Foundation. Used by permission of Tyndale House Publishers, Inc., Carol Stream, Illinois 60188. All rights reserved. Used by permission.

Scriptures marked NIV are taken from the NEW INTERNATIONAL VERSION (NIV): Scripture taken from THE HOLY BIBLE, NEW INTERNATIONAL VERSION ®. Copyright© 1973, 1978, 1984, 2011 by Biblica, Inc.™. Used by permission of Zondervan

Some names and details of stories included in this book have been changed in order to protect individual privacy.

Front cover image by Nicole Voelkel

Text format design by https://usedtotech.com

This book is dedicated to my father, Dave Smith. His obedience to the Voice of God and willingness to walk the talk has set the standard for my life. He lives his life as he pleases. His counter cultural beliefs rub many the wrong way as he truly lives his life for God and doesn't pay too much attention to what people think. Our frequent relocations, hosting guests, taking in foster kids, holding church services in our living room, and lack of materialism have had a lasting impact on my life. He always finds a way to focus on the spiritual over the material as a way of living.

I want to thank my wonderful wife Bogusia and my two children Anette and Josh for their support and patience in the book writing process and their willingness to charge forward on our Journey in Christ.

I would also like to thank Nicole Voelkel for her research, writing, and guidance in the book publishing experience. Without her work, this book would have never been released.

CONTENTS

CHAPTER 1: A FAITH OF LEAP   11

CHAPTER 2: CALLED TO DO THE IMPOSSIBLE   34

CHAPTER 3: HOW TO HEAL SICK PEOPLE   55

CHAPTER 4: MIRACLES IN A CRISIS   75

CHAPTER 5: OVERCOMING POWERS OF DARKNESS   95

CHAPTER 6: SPIRITUAL ATMOSPHERES AND THE POWER OF FORGIVENESS   108

CHAPTER 7: BACKDOORS OF HEAVEN   130

CHAPTER 8: GET OUT OF THE BOAT   149

CHAPTER 9: PRAY FOR THOSE WHO PERSECUTE YOU   169

CHAPTER 10: KNOW YOUR WHY   182

CHAPTER 1: A FAITH OF LEAP

Go out on a limb. That's where the fruit is. — Jimmy Carter

Have you ever wondered if God has more for your life? Are you a career professional that has always focused on doing a good job and being a kind person — but wish you could see Christianity making a bigger difference in a real way in the lives of people around you? Do you believe the Bible is true, but would love to see a miracle with your own eyes?

I was a twelve-year career administrator, a principal in a Chicago school district, when I realized that God was not only still doing miracles every day — the kind that Jesus did, healing the sick and casting out demons — and that he actually wanted to use me to do them. I believe many of us professionals are so trained to separate our personal lives from our professional lives that we too easily forget what it means to keep in step with the Holy Spirit — every second of every day. My life changed when I realized that rather than just praying and asking God to take the problems away, I was actually chosen to be his answer to those problems, to continue doing the things Jesus did in the midst of the normal day-to-day problems that surrounded me.

For a few years I had been listening to teachings and testimonies about how to be used by God, similar to the teaching you will find in this book. Up until that time I had just been going to work as usual, going to church as usual. As I listened, I remember it finally struck me with the profound realization of what it means to truly follow Jesus and do the things that Jesus did. I knew, "This is for me," and in my heart I made a decision that I would be obedient to this even if it was uncomfortable or hard.

A few days later I was walking down the hall of my school, peeking in classrooms and stepping in to encourage our new staff. The smell of glue, sandwiches, and new erasers always made me smile. My thoughts were interrupted when I caught sight of one of my team leaders, Anna, shuffling toward me down the hall, clenching her stomach. I hurried up to her and asked if she was okay. The pain in her eyes was clear, and she sadly mumbled that she really needed to go home, she felt horrible and wasn't able to keep it together anymore. When I talked to her, it felt as if she were suddenly highlighted to me, like someone was holding a lamp behind her. It could have felt like just a random moment, easy to dismiss and move on, but something clicked in my mind that maybe this was actually God trying to get my attention. I think He went to an extreme measure in this case, because He knew how busy and task-oriented I was at school. He was trying to show me that this was a spiritual moment, just like I had been praying for. The problem is, I didn't know what to do, but I did sense God telling me, "Don't procrastinate...it's time to dive in."

I told the teacher to get her stuff to go home and to stop by my office before she left. By the time I returned to my office several other things had come up, and I had forgotten about the incident until I walked through my door. She was sitting there, her coat on and with her packed bags, waiting by my desk. "Oh no," I froze. "She's here. I have to do something, what am I going to do?" I asked her what was going on, stalling as I frantically wondered what I should do. As she described her symptoms to me I suddenly blurted out, "God can heal you."

"WHO??!!!" she asked. This was the first time I had ever mentioned God, and I think we were both just as surprised at what came out of my mouth. I realized neither of us really had any idea about what was going to happen.

I smiled as I explained, "Our God can heal you; would you like to pray with me?" Somewhat quizzically, she nodded in agreement.

As we prayed I felt really strong twinges in my back. That was unusual for me. Since they began just as soon as we started praying I wondered if it might actually be a way that God was speaking to me about what was going on. I described the pain and asked her if she was possibly experiencing something like that. Her eyes grew wide in shock. She shared with me that since she was eight years old she'd had terrible back problems, which began when she used to ride horses. This really encouraged my faith that

God had revealed this pain, and I told her I believed that God was about to heal her. I prayed and asked her how she felt. She exclaimed with great excitement that all the pain had left, and that she was able to do movements with her back that she had been unable to do for years. Her cold symptoms had disappeared by 50%. We prayed again, and they were gone. I explained to her that God had healed her in that moment, and that He wanted her to know that He was real and that He wanted to have a relationship with her.

She asked me, "Well, what do I do?" I told her we could pray together and answer His invitation. Then she asked if she should still go home, since she was completely well. I told her since I already called a sub in, she could just go home and take the day off. She said, "I can't wait to tell my boyfriend, my mom, everyone I know, what just happened to me." That's when I knew it was going to be a wild ride.

I was your typical twelve-year career administrator, a "nice guy" school principal in a midwestern suburb of Chicago, when I realized that God was up to something. Looking at me from the outside, you would see an average American guy with a wife and two kids. We both had professional degrees, solid careers, and a comfortable lifestyle. We tried our best to be good citizens in our community and church, helping out where we could. I figured I was pretty much set to keep this going until retirement. What more could God ask of me? It was at this midpoint in my professional career when I began to realize that the Jesus we see in Scripture is much more powerful and radical than what would fit into the typical American suburban neighborhood, and just maybe

Michael D Smith

He was calling me to walk in His same footsteps as I went about my job, my city, my life.

For the first time, I realized I could pray for people and see God do a miracle on the spot. I grew in confidence and faith as it began to happen on a regular basis, and I watched as the prayers I made in the early morning time with God began to manifest in front of my eyes. We have all things in Christ, and wherever you are in your job, or your career, God has more for you.

My passion is to equip people, especially working professionals in serious careers – to realize that their position is for a purpose. If you have been born again, you have been given power and authority from heaven to see the kingdom of God manifest wherever you go, just like Jesus did. As you read through these pages, I will take you step by step in a process of recognizing your calling, tuning in more clearly to God's guidance throughout the day, stepping out in obedience even when it feels risky, and begin to see the purposes of God unfold powerfully in your life. His power manifests not just through signs and wonders, but in practical wisdom that we see in many biblical examples of men of God who were able to recognize his voice, obey quickly, and administrate the massive moves of God throughout scripture and history.

I believe many of us professionals are so trained to separate our personal lives from our work lives that we easily forget what it means to keep in step with the Holy Spirit. My life took a turning point mid-career when I realized that rather than just praying and asking God to take the problems away, I was actually chosen to be His answer to those problems.

LEAP

WHEN GOD INTERRUPTS US

The first time I felt God pulling at my heart, I was completely clueless. I was in a crowded bar surrounded by laughing people and music so loud I couldn't even hear myself speak. It was 1988, and I was a college student at the top of my game, pledged at one of the elite fraternities on campus. I was young and having a great time, majoring in business with big plans to be successful and make a lot of money. Just like the people around me, we were all focused on networking, becoming as popular as possible, and landing a great job to make us rich. On the surface it looked like everything was what I wanted, I had it all together. We had just thrown a huge party with hundreds of people who were having a great time, and I was at the center of a large group of popular friends who had made it to the top. We were laughing and talking, and as I reached for another glass, a sudden realization swept over me that, actually, I was all alone. In the middle of all the noise and distraction of that moment, it hit me that what I was pursuing was empty, and I thought to myself, "There must be more to life than this." My heart was filled with questions and cried out for something more. It may not have looked like a prayer, but God heard my heart and answered.

The answer came that summer, in the form of a huge Greyhound bus on the way to Monterrey, Mexico. Wiesiek Stebnicki, a Polish missionary I knew, had invited me to be part of a YWAM (Youth With A Mission) group going down to work with the poor, and it sounded interesting to me.

Our ministry was very simple: we were just going house to house in the little neighborhoods, knocking on doors, and telling people about God's love for them and the forgiveness of sins. We also practiced sharing the gospel in the form of a wordless skit that had many symbols of salvation and forgiveness. That same afternoon, a young guy came up to me and said to me in English, "I want what you're talking about." I was confused, and just looked back at him blankly. He pointed to the skits, and said, "I want that."

I thought, "Oh my gosh these skits actually work!" I prayed with him and he received Christ. After the skits were over, we decided to go and pray for people outside of a large Catholic church as mass was ending. A Spanish-speaking girl who was helping our team joined me. She singled out a lady coming out of mass and started talking to her. The woman wasn't able to communicate very well because she was deaf. My friend turned to me and said, "This woman is deaf, so let's pray for her!"

We prayed for her, and all of a sudden her eyes were as wide as saucers, "I can hear! I can hear!" The only thing I knew at that moment was, "Our God is great." The rest of our trip was like that. It was an amazing experience to see so many things happen, but I thought it was something special in that group, at that time. I didn't know that this was normal, this was really the normal way the Christian life was meant to be lived out. To me at that point, prayer still felt more like rolling dice. I didn't understand my role in it.

Even though I had experienced God calling me to serve Him, even specifically to help the people of Mexico, I still sort of lost sight of the original vision and drive to see God move. Over the next few decades I ended up in a career in education and eventually serving the Hispanic population in Chicago, but I still had to reach a point in my life where I again said "Yes" to God, and told Him that I was ready and willing to be used by Him in any way that He wanted. As I began to step into the situations God seemed to put in my path, I began to realize I could pray for people and see God do miracles on the spot. I grew in confidence and faith as it began to happen on a regular basis, and I watched as the prayers I made in the early morning time with God began to manifest in front of my eyes.

God is the same yesterday, today, and tomorrow — and when Jesus came to announce the good news of the kingdom of God, he didn't do it with a bumper sticker on His car. He did it by healing the sick, casting out demons, and seeing people's lives change completely. For years, I had bought into the subtle lie that I couldn't do these kinds of things as a principal. It wouldn't be appropriate, or maybe worse—nothing would happen if I prayed and I would make Christianity seem foolish.

If you have been born again, you have been given power and authority from heaven to see the kingdom of God manifest wherever you go, just like Jesus did. My passion is to help train people, especially professionals working in high-level careers – to realize that their position is for a purpose. As you read through these pages, I will take you step-by-step in a process of recognizing your calling, tuning in more clearly to God's guidance throughout the day, stepping out in obedience even when it feels risky, and beginning to see the purposes of God unfold in your life, not just through signs and wonders, but in practical wisdom and strategies that will impact your community. We see many biblical examples of people of God who were able to recognize His voice, obey quickly, and administrate the massive moves of God throughout Scripture and history.

HOW DOES GOD SPEAK TO US

Sometimes, when we imagine God speaking to someone, we sort of imagine God waking us up in the night with an audible voice telling us what to do. God does sometimes do that, but in Scripture we also see many different creative ways which God speaks to His people throughout history. He speaks through circumstances, other people, Scripture, prayer, visions, audible voice, physical sensations, signs, nature, and even angels. In Jeremiah 18, the Lord used a potter working at his job to give a visual message to Jeremiah. Today, God may even use music or movies to speak to your heart. We serve a God who is constantly speaking to us, though we don't always recognize it immediately.

WHAT IS THE LOVE OF GOD LIKE?

During that first mission trip, we were taught to have quiet times each morning: reading Scripture, praying, and then waiting to listen. This became a lifelong practice for me that God uses time and time again to transform situations around me. During one of those first mornings, I remember walking back to the dorms with a friend after spending time in prayer, asking God to lead me and speak to me.

It was early morning in the desert, the sun was already bright and sweeping out the cool from the night before. In the distance, an arched mountain range showed patches of brush and scorched rock rising up in the heat. I passed by an open field of sand and short yellow grass, and suddenly I felt the presence of God flow around me. It was like liquid love. Immediately a huge weight I didn't even know I was carrying lifted off of my back. I remember thinking, "This is what the love of God is like!" My friend who was with me asked me what was going on, what was the matter. I couldn't even speak to answer him. Instead, I just started sobbing. I realized that this moment was what life was all about. I was meant to know God and to obey Him. He was more real to me than anything else, and finally I said, "Now I know what you guys are talking about. This is the love of God. I'm going to do whatever it takes to follow Him. I don't know what this journey is going to be like, but I just have to pursue it."

I had never known anything like that moment before. I knew what was happening, even though I had never experienced it before. Somehow I recognized that I was in the presence of the Almighty, and I knew I would make whatever changes in my life to do whatever God wanted me to do. I knew this immediately. I couldn't go back to that fraternity house, because if I did, I wouldn't live out my life like a Christian should live. I needed to change everything, even though I didn't know yet what that would look like.

Just like the woman who was healed of deafness, my spiritual ears were beginning to open up to start to recognize and follow God's voice in my life.

In 1 Samuel, Israel is in a situation where things have become a mess. The spiritual leaders are partying and womanizing. They have become corrupt and astray from God's call. In the middle of the night, God wakes Samuel up with an important message, and

Michael D Smith

I believe this encounter is helpful to us for understanding what it looks to like to recognize and respond when God is speaking:

> One night ...Samuel was sleeping in the Tabernacle near the Ark of God. Suddenly the Lord called out, "Samuel!"
> "Yes?" Samuel replied. "What is it?" He got up and ran to Eli. "Here I am. Did you call me?"
> "I didn't call you," Eli replied. "Go back to bed." So he did.
> Then the Lord called out again, "Samuel!"
> Again Samuel got up and went to Eli. "Here I am. Did you call me?"
> "I didn't call you, my son," Eli said. "Go back to bed." Samuel did not yet know the Lord because he had never had a message from the Lord before. So the Lord called a third time, and once more
> Samuel got up and went to Eli. "Here I am. Did you call me?"
> Then Eli realized it was the Lord who was calling the boy. So he said to Samuel, "Go and lie down again, and if someone calls again, say, 'Speak, Lord, your servant is listening.'"
> 1 Samuel 3:2-10 (NIV)

God is always speaking to us, but sometimes it's difficult for us to recognize His voice and be confident that it's actually God speaking to us. Even though God was audibly speaking to Samuel, it actually took him three times to recognize God's voice. Many of us assume that if God would just clearly speak to us, it would be easy to understand what He wants us to do, but in this example from Scripture we see that was not the case. The truth is, God is speaking clearly to us, but it's us who must learn to recognize His voice and the way that He is speaking to us. This comes with practice over time, but it's one of the most important parts of learning to follow Christ.

In John 10:27 (BLB), Jesus says, "My sheep hear My voice, I know them, and they follow Me." Sometimes as Christians we fear it would be arrogant or presumptive for someone to say that God spoke to us, but it's very biblical. Even sheep can recognize the voice of their shepherd, because they spend time with him every day. We can take that same humble position as a sheep. Hearing God's voice doesn't depend on having a great prophetic gift, or being a great saint of God, but it simply comes from spending time with God every day, even in the simple things of life. A good shepherd knows how to guide his sheep and lead them. If they make a mistake, he is able to help them back on the right path.

During my mission trip with YWAM, I was fortunate to be trained to put this into practice on a daily basis. As we spend time in God's word, we become familiar with His voice. Each morning I would spend 5-10 minutes reading God's word, 5-10 minutes praying, and 5-10 minutes simply listening and writing down what I sensed He was saying. Many Christians spend time praying, but don't take time to sit quietly and listen to God. As you create a regular space in your life to listen to God, He will guide you, drop things into your spirit, bring Scriptures and ideas, even images to your mind. We can't assume that everything we sense is from God, but by quietly listening and noticing, we will start to recognize how God speaks to us, and those things He says will bear fruit in our life.

Michael D Smith

Many of us are aware of the need for daily quiet time for our personal life, but a significant turning point comes when we start to apply this kind of mindset to our workplace. During my trip with YWAM, I saw God do amazing things on the mission field, but it wasn't until more than a decade later that I started to see the same things happen in my workplace on a daily basis.

The first school I taught at was a very challenging Title I school in inner-city Chicago. One day I was telling my principal about the serious problems I was having with students who had horrible things going on at home and were constantly acting out in the classroom. She surprised me with a question. "Do you pray for your kids, Mike?" I kind of looked at her and shrugged. Of course, I went to church and I *prayed*...but it was more of a general thing.

She said, "Listen, you should really be praying for all of these kids. You have no idea what is going on in their lives and what God wants to do to touch them during their time here. None of this stuff is coincidence, God has you here for a reason."

"But what about separation of church and state?" I asked her. "I don't want to get fired."

My principal said, "You have to remember who got you that job. We answer to One who is greater than the one that signs the paycheck. This is in a poor neighborhood in gangland in Chicago. These kids have very little going for them, and you are their only hope, and what hope do you have that is greater than what God can do?"

My principal had the expectation that I would be praying for each of my students, their families, and the neighborhood. I had the sense that she even thought I should be praying for them in person. Prior to that, I had been in the mentality that church was what I did for fun, outside of my job, but that at my job I just needed to be a good employee, and that was how I showed my Christianity. Her perspective was a unique one, because she opened my eyes to the need around me and showed me that I was part of God's answer.

She planted an important seed in my life that shifted the way I viewed my job. It was still several years before my theology shifted to the point where I began realizing God could use me to do miracles on the spot, but I took to heart what she said about the need for God to intervene in students' lives. At that time, I began coming in early to lay hands on each of the chairs in my classroom, praying over each of the kids by name, praying for the lessons I taught each day, and praying for their families.

In the book of Samuel, he had been faithfully serving as an assistant in the temple, and God chose to tell him what he was about to do. In this case, Samuel had been serving under corrupt leadership, but he was serving faithfully. God saw his actions, and his heart. I believe it's significant that his first response to God was, "Speak, Your servant is listening."

Without yet knowing what God would ask of him, his heart was positioned to obey. Many times I believe when our hearts become hardened by continuing doing our own will, it creates a spiritual hardness of hearing. For example, Eli's sons were corrupt and self-serving in their personal and professional lives. Even though they were appointed to hear God's voice and lead the Israelites, God overstepped their position in favor of someone whose life was already inclined toward obedience. I believe as we surrender our daily choices and actions toward holiness and obedience of God's word, it sensitizes us toward helping us hear His voice as well, even when we least expect it – in the middle of our "busiest" days, to surprise us. Starting to see God's power in my workplace has often started with a willingness to override my own agenda.

DIVINE DISTRACTIONS
There was a mother in our school district who had a lot of problems, and who was regularly coming to our office for support. Her husband was on disability and just sat at home smoking weed all day long. All of her kids were gangbangers in the neighborhood and her grandkids were constantly having issues in our school. I was having an extremely hectic day, and when I heard her talking to our front secretaries, I honestly was hoping she might pass by without coming in to talk to me. Instead she decided to drop in and chat for a while. I kept eyeing the stack of things on my desk that needed to be finished that afternoon, wishing her visit would end quickly. Several times she mentioned how much her fingers were hurting from carpal tunnel syndrome. She told me that the repetition she did at work was causing her a lot of pain. It crossed my mind that I could pray for her, but basically I ignored that feeling because I was too busy that day. I had a meeting coming up I still needed to prepare for. Finally, I dismissed her and told her I really needed to get going.

For some reason she still wouldn't leave but hung around, almost as if she was waiting for something from me. I finally sent her on her way, and she politely left. As soon as she walked out the door, the Holy Spirit told me, "You really missed that opportunity." It hit me like a ton of bricks. Here I had been praying for God to please break into my life with the supernatural ministry of Jesus, but I was pushing away the opportunities that came right to me. What could I do? I realized that my office had a side door that the mother had to walk out to leave the building. I rushed to cut her off before she reached the school entrance. She looked up, and I blurted out, "Hey, you know about your fingers? God can heal you."

She seemed a little taken aback, but answered, "Yeah, well, I suppose." I asked her if she wanted to come in and I could pray for healing. She said, "Not now, I really have a lot of things to do." Ironically, those were the same words I had been giving to her for the past half hour as I tried to push her on her way, and now she used them back at me.

"Oh, come on," I urged her, "It will take two minutes." She reluctantly agreed, and I could tell my secretaries were really surprised to see her walking back in with me. As soon as we prayed, the pain went from a level ten in the middle finger to zero. In her index finger the pain went from a level ten to three. She started to cry. When she was crying, I asked her if she could feel that presence of peace that was with us. She nodded yes. It was a holy moment, a special touch from the Holy Spirit who was pouring out His compassion and love on this woman whose life was very difficult and full of pain. We serve a gracious God, who is tenderhearted and close to the weary-hearted. I believe she felt the Holy Spirit, and she didn't know what to make of it.

We prayed again for the last twinge of pain in her finger, and I told her Jesus loves her and wants a relationship with her. She didn't want to pray to receive Jesus right then, but I explained how to do it later on her own, what it would be like. She was really touched and encouraged by the experience, and left the office beaming. God is a God of second chances. He is gracious and compassionate, and He loves people so much he is even willing to use us to reach them, even if we are busy, and even if we miss it the first time.

When I shared that story with my brother-in-law in Chicago, he told me how that created a chain reaction in his life. He owned a roofing company, and he was at one of his locations in Chicago getting permits. While he was working on that, a FedEx guy showed up to make a delivery and ended up telling him about his recent divorce, and opening up with a lot of personal information about the hard time he was going through. My brother-in-law cut the conversation short and dismissed the guy because he needed to get back on the job. The guy finally left, and as my brother-in-law got back in the car and started pulling away, he suddenly remembered that story I told him about the woman at my school. The guy was gone and he didn't know how to find him again so he called me up and asked me, "What can I do now?" He was never in that part of town and the chances of him seeing the same FedEx guy again would be really remote. We prayed and asked God to set up another meeting with that guy. At the next family function, he said, "You're not going to believe what happened!" He was out shopping for supplies at Home Depot in a completely different part of Chicagoland, and ended up bumping into the same guy in the store. "Hey, how are you doing?" he asked the guy. He ended up praying with him right there in the store, and the man was crying. God is so much bigger than we can imagine. Sometimes I think He is laughing in heaven, enjoying surprising us as we realize that he is bigger than we could imagine.

The Holy Spirit can communicate to us in many ways, through Scripture, dreams, through conversations with other people. Sometimes He uses repetition of certain numbers or visual cues to get our attention. Sometimes when I'm looking at a crowd, or a situation, all of a sudden someone's image becomes clearer, it's like they become highlighted to me. God communicates in different ways for different people. And I'm thankful that He does this for me, otherwise I think I would miss things, because naturally I get so focused on my tasks and finishing what I'm doing that I am not very aware when these things happen. A lot of times the Holy Spirit will correct me later and show me that I really missed a moment. It's important to set aside time daily to pray and ask God to use us. Over the years He has often shown me things just before they happen, given me certain premonitions to prepare ahead of time, or brought things into the light that help me protect my school and lead well. God is at work in our lives every day and in the lives of those around us. Setting aside time to seek Him, and tune into His voice through prayer and Scripture, will start to make this more obvious, as you recognize confirmations that happen throughout the day.

I believe that the enemy tries to spread the lie that if we truly follow God, our lives will become very boring. Nothing could be farther from the truth. "See, I am doing a new thing! Now it springs up; do you not perceive it? I am making a way in the wilderness and streams in the wasteland." (Isaiah 43:19 NIV). This is the God of the universe, who never makes two snowflakes the same. It's important for us to tune into God on a regular basis, because it allows us to become part of His creative plan. Your workplace may be the last place you think God would want to show up, but that is not the case. Samuel was serving in a temple where things were going very poorly. Corruption and abuse of power were happening all around him. He might have felt hopeless, resentful or embittered that his life had been dedicated to serving people who were doing a terrible job in their office. Actually, God was about to change all of that. The Scriptures tell us in the first part of 2 Chronicles 16:9 (NLT), "The eyes of the LORD search the whole earth in order to strengthen those whose hearts are fully committed to him." Rather than falling into the trap of rebellion or bad-talking, Samuel's heart remained steadfast, and, in the right time, God used him for a mighty purpose in Israel.

When God spoke to Samuel, it lined up with the word that God had already spoken. God's word to you will be in line with Scripture. Significantly, Samuel then shared this word with his spiritual mentor, who was also able to affirm that the word was from God (even though it was against his own self-interest!). The Lord also called out to Samuel three times with His message. Many times when I am listening to God's voice about a major decision or move, I'll look for these same kinds of confirmations in Scripture, through other Christians, and through a repetition of the message. Over the years I have developed a habit that when I sense God's presence, like He is beginning to stir something in the atmosphere, I will literally throw up my hands in the air and say out loud, "Speak, Lord, your servant is listening." I want to cultivate that practice to be ready and available to respond outside of my comfort zone or complacency. Sometimes we get very worried wondering, "Did I hear God right, or was that just me?"

One thing I have noticed over the years is that the word of God bears fruit. Even though He can direct us to do challenging or difficult things, it's often accompanied by a sense of peace, joy, grace, and provision. As I step forward to obey God, I've seen doors open in unusual ways, and I've seen that He is faithful to empower us with what we need to accomplish the task. If we make a mistake, or misunderstand the details, He is big enough and powerful enough to steer us back on track. The important thing is that our hearts are attentive, our character is faithful, and we are willing to obey. With those three things in place, God is able to do incredible things far beyond our own capacity even to imagine.

We serve a creative God, and even if you have bounced around between different jobs or different careers, I am convinced that God wastes nothing. As you begin to lean into His plans and purposes for you on a daily basis, you will see how truly all things have been working together for the good of those that love Him – for your good, and for the people that He brings into your schedule each day when you least expect it. Besides sharing stories and testimonies of what God has shown me is possible for us to live in the middle of our busy work week, I will also give practical exercises and show you how to take the first step. This kind of mentoring was key for my life, and I hope it will be an encouragement to you in the mission that God has you on. May today be the first day of a radical new understanding of what it means to be a Christ-follower.

SUMMARY
In this chapter I shared significant turning points in my understanding of what it means to follow Christ, not just to pray for God's intervention in difficult situations, but to BECOME God's intervention. Learning to respond to God's voice in our life is an important part of this. In the life of Samuel, we learn key principles for hearing God's voice:
- o practice spending time with God regularly
- o a willingness to obey
- o faithfulness to a Godly character and lifestyle despite the actions or sin of people around us
- o checking for congruency with Scripture
- o confirmation from other believers/mentors
- o and the Word bearing fruit in our life

REFLECTION
During this chapter I share a progression of significant turning points in my life. Was there a time when you could relate to any of the following moments in my story?
- o Being a busy and distracted college student, being self-focused?
- o Being on a spiritual high like a mission trip, wanting to give your life to Christ?
- o Stepping out and taking a risk for God, even if it didn't make sense?

Take a few minutes to sketch out your own "timeline," listing at least six moments of either spiritual highs or lows. Where would you say you are at now?

As you look back over that timeline, what ways has God used most often to speak to you? Circle any of the following examples you have experienced.

Scripture   Nature People Circumstances Dreams Visions
Repeated Instances   Prayer   Audible Voice
Peace   Popping Words Popping Images
Supernatural Manifestations   Movie/Media   Music
Numbers   Prophetic Ministry   Angelic visitations

ACTIVATION
Commit this week to spending 15 minutes each morning with God – five minutes reading the Bible, five minutes praying, and at least five minutes of those simply listening, and then writing down any impression you have that He could be saying to you.

HOW TO HAVE YOUR QUIET TIMES
Quiet times should have three parts. If you're not doing anything at all, then start by setting your alarm fifteen minutes earlier than usual.
- o Get up, go to your favorite place, read your Bible for five minutes. (I use the Discipleship Journal by NAVPRESS Bible in A Year, free download from Navigators website.)

o   Pray: tell God all the things that are on your heart, like a one-way conversation, even though He knows all these things, let Him know that you recognize these things.

o   Sit for five minutes and ask, "God what are You speaking to me?" Be aware of any thoughts you are getting. Be aware of any feelings or ideas that are coming to you. This is when you are able to listen and receive. Even if you are not feeling anything, keep doing it. You will never go wrong by reading His word. If five minutes isn't enough for praying, then give yourself more time.

The more you do it, you'll find you'll have more to pray about, you'll want to read more, and you'll want to be in His presence more. You will never go wrong doing those three things. Have faith that our God is big and He wants a relationship with you. As you set that time apart, you will see God move. (Any one of those three things is good, but combined, it's a package that can be life-changing.)

LEAP

CHAPTER 2: CALLED TO DO THE IMPOSSIBLE

I am always doing that which I cannot do, in order that I may learn how to do it. — Pablo Picasso

Sofia, a tiny second grader with a thick, dark ponytail and disheveled clothes, stood with hands on her hips screaming in front of the stairs. For more than a month, this girl refused to enter the school building. Each day her parents would try to drop her off, and each day she would scream at the top of her voice for her mother. We, as a school, had set up a social worker and gotten counseling for her family. When we finally got her in the class, she would continue screaming for an hour straight, completely disturbing everyone else in the room. I put her in my office for the whole morning and gave her to another teacher to look after her in the afternoon. I called a meeting with her parents, and both mom and dad showed up. In my mind, I wasn't going to kick this girl out of school, but technically I had to explain how progressive discipline worked. When I was done talking to them, I prayed for the Holy Spirit to give me wisdom, and then I waited. What came to my mind right away was that I should ask the mother if she had spoken to the priest. The girl's teacher who was in the meeting with me looked at me, shocked, as I steered off the standard protocol.

The mother shook her head, but confirmed that she had been thinking of doing that for some time now. Just before this happened, a "missionary" from Mexico had come to their house and had done some rituals on their daughter. The mother told me that the girl picked up a bad spirit in the school bathroom when the kids were doing Bloody Mary, a game of calling down powers. I told her to go see Father Dave at Our Lady of Good Counsel Church and I asked her permission that if anything else happened at school, would I be able to pray with her daughter if she was sent to my office again? I reassured them that within a week, it would all be taken care of. After the parents left, the teacher was incredulous at how smoothly we had seemed to come into agreement.

"But how on earth did you know to ask about the priest?"

I told her, "Sometimes I know things." I didn't share more openly then, but was starting to notice that when I would stop and ask the Spirit for wisdom, He would often give me very specific responses that saved a lot of time and often surprised even me. This teacher was a New Age Mexican-American who mixed Mayan shamanism with some traditional Catholicism. From that point on, she seemed to regard me as somewhat of a mystic-healer, and she began regularly calling me to deal with student families when she sensed there could be some spiritual issues involved, or situations that were complex.

A few days later, the same girl was brought into my office by another teacher because she was so full of anxiety that she wouldn't go into the classroom. This girl had become a completely different person than the sweet little girl we knew from the year before, and I sensed it was a spiritual issue at play. Since her parents had given me permission to pray with her, I explained to the girl how Jesus can take away our fears. I asked the girl if she wanted to invite Jesus into her heart, and she answered, "Yes," she wanted that. We guided the girl into a prayer of salvation, and she began to feel tingling in her hands.

I reached out again to Father Dave, the local Spirit-filled Catholic priest. He had been referred to me as a great local resource who was well respected in the community, being very sensitive to spiritual issues and knowing how to minister to them. He let me know that a woman from Mexico had shown up in Aurora, going to all the home groups, telling people that she was a missionary. But in the groups this woman visited, bad things had started happening. This woman soon disappeared, but Father Dave was doing a lot of clean-up work from her activities. When the woman visited the home group, that's when things started with this little girl.

After the little girl invited Jesus into her heart, she became a completely changed person. She sat quietly in the front of her class, working diligently and politely asking questions in a hushed whisper. In fact, her parents had been separated, on the verge of divorce, but after seeing their daughter delivered from these spirits and meeting with the priest, the entire family ended up receiving Christ. None of the staff at the school could believe the change they saw take place with the student. The girl started coming to school primly dressed to the nines, and gently asking the teacher if it would be okay to start each day in prayer. Just the week before, she had been terrorizing the classroom. This New Age teacher brought the girl to my office and asked me to pray with her before they started their day. We knelt down and prayed on our knees, in classic catechism style. She knew something had changed drastically, and that opened the door to more that God wanted to do in her life.

When we place our hearts and our lives fully in His hands and let the Holy Spirit begin to rest in us, there is no limit to what God is able to do through our lives. It might be on the world stage or it might be in a place of hiddenness. With each person I meet in my school, from the students to the faculty, I know God loves them and has a plan for their life. Like this little girl, many of them have suffered extreme brokenness, abandonment, and entered into a lifestyle of self-harm. From an outside perspective, there wasn't much hope for the kids in the East Aurora school district. High poverty, high crime, homelessness, drug addiction, gang affiliations— It wasn't exactly a school district people would be proud of. As I myself began to step into this journey of listening to the Holy Spirit and giving Him full permission to use me as He sees fit, I was amazed at how I began to see the kingdom of God – the Shalom of Heaven – begin to break into even simple, everyday situations: healing lives, restoring faith, and watching our community start to bloom again.

The Bible tells us that with the faith of a mustard seed, we can move mountains. As each of us is called to faith, I believe that God plants those mustard seeds with a promise to move mountains. Within each salvation prayer is a promise to see the Kingdom of God, the Hebrew *Shalom*, that is a promise of transformation, not only of individual lives, but families, communities, cities, and an entire nation. In my own life, I believe that the "mustard seed" of faith was planted two decades before, when He first called me back to Christ on the mission trip to Mexico.

During the 36-hour bus ride from Chicago to Monterrey the team had developed a nonstop prayer chain that lasted through the night. Groups of students would be heard quietly murmuring prayers in the darkness for 15-20 minutes then pass the prayer on to the next row of seats to intercede for the trip. I had grown up going to a Catholic elementary school, but had never done anything like this before. It seemed like a good idea. At some point during the night just before we got to Mexico, it was my turn to pray. As I bowed my head to pray I suddenly heard the clear loud voices of kids behind me, calling to me to help them. "Come help me, come help me!" I wondered if there were middle schoolers on the bus playing a game. I turned around and looked all around the bus, but the middle schoolers were earnestly praying. As I peered over the seats, I just saw the huddled groups of the YWAM team, praying hushed tones in darkness. My eyes strained back in the darkness, trying to understand. Finally, I shook my head in curiosity, and then dismissed it. It didn't "fit" with what seemed logical.

Actually, it wasn't until more than a year after the trip, when I was falling back into a routine of work, I heard the Holy Spirit say, "What you heard behind you on the bus to Monterrey was the mountains of Mexico crying out to you." It was a mixture between a voice and instantaneous knowledge, and it re-awakened the sense of God's calling in my life, and it excited me. Over the next few years I tried in my own way to make this happen, learning Spanish, dropping out of college and moving down to Guatemala on a whim, working odd jobs and flipping cars to make money. To be honest, a lot of those projects felt like failure. In my mid-twenties, I finally went back to school to finish a degree in education, figuring it would allow me to travel in the summers. I ended up landing a job teaching in a Chicagoland neighborhood that was 90% Hispanic, and it was actually there that God would again re-awaken me to His call over my life.

Many times, God plants seeds in our life that fully manifest after we have matured and grown into God's timing for our life. By the time I had earned my second Master's degree in Chicago in administration, I had become well-networked within Chicago public schools and had landed a very comfortable position working down at Central office where my friend was appointed to the Board of Education. The original sense of urgency and mission had faded into the background, after several "failed" attempts when I had tried to make it happen on my own effort and imagination. In the meantime, I had started getting involved in the political aspect of education, being invited to meet such dignitaries as the Mexican diplomat and being treated like part of the Insiders' Circle, meeting lots of movers and shakers in education. I met and married my wife and was busy all of the time at school, taking classes, and working out at the health club. I was starting to realize that I could probably make a pretty good career in education, but somewhere in my heart I felt like I was starting to lose the focus of why I started teaching in the first place: the connection I would feel when I met with the families, especially the Mexican immigrant populations in Chicago who were often left out on many levels. There was a disconnect between my head and my heart. I was questioning my faith that God could still use me to do the impossible, as I had seen as a young man. I was successful by the world's standards. On the outside it looked like I had become a rising star, but on the inside, I was beginning to have doubts again as to whether I was really fulfilling those dreams God had given me as a twenty-year-old.

Six months later, a newly-elected superintendent closed down my department, and I was out of a job. In my times of prayer, I began asking God, "Why would you do this to me? Why did you promote me to this position, then take it away? Where do you want me to go from here? I went to many interviews, but nothing stood out to me of interest. Rather than focusing on a job, I started to realize that God must be up to something, and I began praying for Him to show me what His greater purpose was for me. Finally, after a few weeks of praying and searching for jobs, I was sitting at my desk looking at job openings, when I felt Him answer my questions with a question. It was the last week of my current position, and I felt like I heard the Holy Spirit ask me, "What is it that **you** want to do?"

Michael D Smith

It was a question that made me realize that what I really wanted was impossible — I'd love to be both a part-time assistant principal, as well as a part-time ESL teacher, working directly with first-generation kids from Mexico. The chances of one position combining both of these was highly unlikely, because you need both the Administrative certificate and also the specialized teaching certificate, from two completely different fields of study. If I could continue doing what I loved in both of these different streams, it would be my dream job, but I knew it was improbable that anything like that existed. Nothing like that was available in Chicago. Finally, I did a casual Google search for Hispanic populations in Illinois, and Aurora popped up. There were two main school districts and in the Mexican neighborhood of east Aurora, I found a district position for .5 Assistant principal / .5 teacher. It was like throwing a dart on a map and landing in the middle of the ocean, then realizing that in that exact spot was an island with your name on it. I knew in my heart that this was no coincidence. I believe that God had closed down that entire Chicago system education department just to get me into that job. The mountains of Mexico had called me back to my original purpose.

I jumped in my car the next day and drove to Aurora. The offices were closed, but I knocked on the door of the school, and the principal opened the door. The moment I saw her, I knew that I was going to learn a lot from this woman, and that she was going to be an excellent mentor for me. She was counter-cultural and was on a mission to see transformation come to that neighborhood in East Aurora.

Aurora had been an industrial and manufacturing powerhouse up through the 1970s when the railroad centers had closed. Like many other industrial cities in the Midwest, they faced severe decline, with factories and businesses closing for good, and unemployment reaching 16%. By the 80s and 90s the neighborhood crime rates had soared and several large gangs started to take over the streets, especially the Latin Kings. The neighborhood had become mostly poor Hispanics working low-income jobs in the remaining factories. Families and businesses fled to wealthier suburbs, while the city's murder rate had risen to three times the national rate, hitting 26 murders in 1996 and 25 murders in 2002. Students and teachers at my school told me stories of hiding inside their homes in the late afternoon, and of being afraid of getting hit in a drive-by shooting. The playgrounds were empty in a town known for gang activity, open-air drug market, and streets where prostitutes walked in broad daylight picking up work. It was a challenging school district with a lot of needs.

By working in very poor neighborhoods for more than a decade now, I had slowly become desensitized to the needs of broken families and students around me. Many times when we are confronted with the hurts of other people, they come in a form that is alienating and difficult— the parent that cusses out their teacher week after week, while her son is beating up other students in the playground— the family whose kids are failing out of every class, and yet only show up a few days a week to school. It's tempting to become judgmental and irritated in areas where you see people making poor decisions again and again. I tried to do my best to provide a quality education and motivating students to learn, and as an administrator coaching my teachers to become the best educators possible, but it was tiring. It's a challenging task to do well, let alone move beyond that to take on the problems of the surrounding community. I am happy to say that as I gave over the reins to God, I began seeing ripples of impact and lives changed in ways that I never imagined was possible, and it stirred my faith to not give up on this little corner of the world that God had put me in.

For two years I worked as an assistant principal, learning the ins and outs of the job, the right attitude to have with the Central Office, how to get things done, and who were the important allies in making things happen. At the same time, I had begun noticing a little corner church meeting in a three-story wooden house, "Vineyard Aurora." I still was involved in my life back in our upscale neighborhood of North Chicago, yet each time I drove past this church, I kept getting the feeling that I needed to stop and visit. As I walked in the door I realized why: I sensed the Holy Spirit saying, "This is your home."

I started sitting in the back on Sundays. The pastor, Robby Dawkins, was a fiery preacher who taught us about our spiritual gifts and told us regularly that God wanted to use us to do the works of Jesus. He told us to stop asking God to heal people. Instead, he told us that Jesus died so that we would live Spirit-filled lives, full of authority and power to carry out the ministry of Jesus and bring the kingdom of heaven to a hurting and broken world around us. He did frequently lead mission teams down to Latin America, but he also lived out this mission every day in the neighborhood. He would go into biker bars and out into the streets to pray for people. He always prayed for the sick to be healed, and shared the gospel with gang leaders, praying for them to experience the Holy Spirit. A lot of them were touched by God and changed their lives. In fact, our church became filled with ex-Latin King members, famous drug dealers in the area, and prostitutes who used to work in our city. His ministry was having a big impact on the community, and what stood out to me was that he was teaching and training everyone in his church to do the same. During this time, God began to reconnect me to see the purpose in my job, stirring that initial call that I had responded to give Him my whole life. I believe that as we begin to live out of our purpose, we move from survival or success to a life of significance—the life you are meant to live.

From Genesis to Revelation, we see the unfurling of God's mission in the world, His redemption of a fallen universe where sin has devastated not only the human soul, but also the body, family relationships, cities, government injustices, and the environment. Throughout the Old Testament, God makes a covenant with a people through which He promises that all the nations of the earth will be reconciled, with the coming of a Prince of Peace, God's humble servant, who will bring about the promised Shalom of God, and restore all things to Himself.

American theologian Cornelius Plantinga summarizes the Old Testament concept of shalom as this: "The webbing together of God, humans, and all creation in justice, fulfillment, and delight is what the Hebrew prophets call *shalom*. We call it 'peace,' but it means far more than mere peace of mind or a cease-fire between enemies. In the Bible, *shalom* means universal flourishing, wholeness and delight – a rich state of affairs in which natural needs are satisfied and natural gifts fruitfully employed, a state of affairs that inspires joyful wonder as its Creator and Savior opens doors and welcomes the creatures in whom he delights. *Shalom*, in other words, is the way things ought to be."[1]

Jesus came teaching and demonstrating an upside-down kingdom like nothing the world had ever seen. The King washed the feet of His servants. The innocent faith of little children received the highest honor as the example to imitate. The leprous, blind, diseased beggars were healed by the King himself. I imagined the homeless folks that I passed every day in Chicago being set free and invited in to join the most exquisite wedding feast. The women that everyone else rejected as broken, slutty and unwanted, became the ones to anoint and honor the Lord of the universe.

Uneducated, simple men from a forgotten fishing village became world class heroes who would speak before kings and empires, perform astounding miracles, travel across empires, be martyred for their faith and change history forever. The kingdom of God is a mighty force that transforms everything it touches. Jesus compares it to yeast, a seemingly simple, almost invisible ingredient — but within a few hours it transforms the whole dough, anywhere it's added.

Sometimes with God's promises, you "put them in the ground" because you don't know what else to do with them — it may even feel like you're giving up on them, but they are still fully alive and waiting to spring up when the temperature and soil is right. I went through many different phases in my journey. It's important to trust and have the faith that everything in our life can be used by God, for His purposes. A major transition happened for me when I realized that the same God I saw as a twenty-year-old healing deaf ears in Mexico was with me when I walked down the halls of my school. God was finally opening my eyes to realize that all around me there were a lot of people walking around in darkness and hopelessness. Because of the Holy Spirit and all the authority that has been given over to Christ, we are actually able to do something about it, much beyond what we could ever do in our own capacity. I began to realize that the job that God had given me was not just His way of providing **for** me, but it was His way of providing **through** me to others around me. Maybe it was even His primary purpose in giving me that job.

I believe that for every single person reading this book, God has an incredible plan and purpose for your life, in whatever occupation, country, or situation you find yourself. I have noticed that God often lays the groundwork for this purpose even before we were born. More than twenty years ago, a desperate teenager hated her life, and thought she would be better off dead. Abandoned by her dad, she grew up molested by many men that came in and out of her mom's life. She made a plan to kill herself and even went through with it. She woke up in the hospital room and realized that she was alive. As a five-year-old she had gone to Sunday school with a friend and given her life to Christ. That day in the hospital room, she realized Jesus was there with her, and He was real. She found a church where people loved her and tried to start her life over. A few months later, she became pregnant with an ex-boyfriend and was terrified that everyone at the church would judge her and reject her. She planned to abort the baby, but that week in church someone gave her a prophetic word that God loved her child and had a plan for her life. The church helped her as a single mom, and prophesied over her son that he was a leader in his generation, one who would take back the arts for God. Within a few years, her son became known around the world as Justin Bieber. His mother is Pattie Mallette. I believe many times it's the most "hopeless" cases, the most "hopeless" situations, through which God is actually poised to accomplish some of His greatest missions. It's His revenge on the kingdom of darkness, and He's looking for people to join in His great redemption story.

VISIONS IN THE NIGHT
During a training meeting at our church, we had a special guest preacher from Australia, Kirk Delaney. He was sharing about unusual encounters he had had with God that empowered him to step out with greater faith to see God move. He invited anyone in the church who wanted to receive dreams and visions from God to put out their hands. I looked around the church and noticed that almost nobody had their hands out. "That's odd," I thought to myself. "This is a really big deal. I wonder why more people aren't getting this. Maybe they just don't understand his accent?" Kirk prayed that we would receive seven nights of dreams and visions from God. That night at two in the morning, I woke up and could feel God's presence in the room. I was so tired that I fell back asleep. The second night again, I woke up at two in the morning and felt that God was there, waiting for me. In my sleep I thought, "I don't have time for this," and rolled back over. The third night I

was sleeping soundly and woke up suddenly at two in the morning.

Again, I was about to fall asleep when I felt like the Holy Spirit spoke to me, "Hey, wait a minute, you're the one that asked for this."

This time I put my hands in the air and began to pray, "Speak to me, speak to me." I had a pad of paper next to my bed and began to write things down, and for the next five days He spoke to me every night, at two in the morning. Each night I wrote everything down, and on the eighth day, it stopped.

When God's presence came into my room, I kept getting a vision of when I was a young Bible school student, a few years after giving my life to Christ. I used to wake up at four in the morning to go pray in the garden outside my dorm and then go back to bed. I remember the closeness I felt with God during those times. So many mornings I remember praying, "Here I am, God, use me, send me where You want."

As I watched myself in the vision, I began crying. I could feel God beside me, showing me myself as a twenty-year-old, and saying, "I was there with you when you were praying and I heard you. I have prepared you, and now is the answer to the time that you were praying for." I realized that it had been exactly twenty years since I was in that Garden.

When we are young with nothing to lose, it's sometimes easier to make those kinds of commitments, and jump into the kind of leap of faith that trusts only in God. As we get older and busier, it takes a more intentional effort to let ourselves get "off track" with our busy schedule, commitments, and how we feel comfortable letting God work.

I remember that at that particular moment in my life I had been feeling really discouraged, like things were going exactly the opposite of the way they should be happening. But suddenly I had the realization that God had been guiding and steering me all along, to where I was in a position to bring a proclamation and demonstration of His message and His kingdom. I knew I wanted to respond, and I trusted that He would use my life as I offered it to Him, even in the little one-mile radius He had placed me. Later on, I would realize it was a much bigger radius than I could imagine.

Each morning as I unlocked the doors of the school, I would pray and ask the Holy Spirit to come and fill our building. I had started a habit each morning of walking the whole school before 8 a.m., praying through each of the halls and spaces of our building and greeting every person. I poked my head in the office of the parent liaison, and right away I could tell she was really sick. She had been sick before Christmas break and I could tell she was still feeling terrible. In fact, she was on her computer looking for a new doctor, and she had been vomiting the past few days.

Right then I realized this was a Holy Spirit moment. She had seen me pray for many families and school staff in our office, but had always kept her distance. "God can heal you," I offered. "Would you like me to pray?" In desperation she nodded yes, and I encouraged her just to receive. I sat down next to her desk and prayed: "Thank you for healing, thank you for caring about your child. Manifest presence of the Holy Spirit, come down and touch her." I could feel God's presence there with us, and I looked up at her, wondering if she could feel it too. Then I saw that tears were streaming down her face, and it looked like she was almost sobbing. I prayed for healing and prayed for her stress. I told her that God loves her and wants a relationship with her. As soon as I started leading her in a prayer inviting God into her life, the intercom started calling her name. I buzzed the office and told them she would come over in a few moments, but the intercom continued calling for her. Despite the distractions and pulls of life around her, she dedicated her life to Christ. She still wasn't feeling that great, but I told her she would be better by lunch and around 11 a.m., she walked into my office with a huge smile announcing that she was finally feeling good. From that moment on she started bringing people to me for prayer as well.

It was the middle of winter, below zero degrees Fahrenheit in Aurora, Illinois, when I saw a woman buzzing at our door. She was nine months pregnant and barely dressed for the freezing weather, just wearing a thin long-sleeve sweater. She had been walking through the neighborhood and became so cold that she came to our school to get warm for a few minutes. We gave her coffee and asked if we could help her with anything. In the meantime, my two secretaries were running around trying to get clothes for this woman. One of my teachers was her size, and she gave her her own winter coat.

Many of the immigrants that ended up in East Aurora came from warm climates and were completely unprepared for the cold. In addition to this, they may be used to having large support systems of family and friends from the towns and villages that they came from, and suddenly found themselves alone in a strange country, unable to speak the language, without knowing how to get help. Two weeks later, a mother walked in with two young boys with just t-shirts on. She said, "I just got off the plane from Mexico. We didn't know this cold existed. We are homeless but trying to get a place in this neighborhood." Immediately everyone started scrambling and making phone calls, trying to get coats and backpacks and clothes for these twin boys.

We got them registered to come to classes starting the next week. She showed up on Monday, later in the day, without the two boys. She had the coats and backpacks. She said, "You know we actually got an apartment in a different neighborhood, so I wanted to return these things since we are not going to your school." She was so honorable, she wanted to give everything back, not realizing that we were giving her those things to keep, not just because her students were coming to our school. At that point I realized, "That's it! We need to step up our game on this." We as a school had an important role as first responders to many of these children and families. Immediately I went and cleared out a storage closet. We were going to keep this stocked with cold-weather blankets and clothing that people would need who would have nothing. We collected so many things for the closet that we ended up having to donate things at the end of the week. That was the time that I made a mental connection that we not only have a part to play in this community, but this is also part of the *Shalom* of God being extended into every realm of the globe, not just useful for dealing with spiritual needs around us but physical as well.

I was helping the Mexican people, not in the way I had pictured, but God had so much more in mind than what I was picturing. I thought I was going to go and work in an orphanage, and that would have made some difference, but what God had in mind was at a much higher level to affect more people in a greater area. I wasn't ready for it, at that time, but later in life when one day I was reviewing my notes of the names of people who were getting saved, I realized all the names were Hispanic, Mexican, and almost all of them were from the area of Durango. It is important not getting discouraged when things don't work out for you the way that you think it should or when it should. A powerful book, *The Modern Schoolhouse*, describes the important effect this has across school systems and changing education. It was written specifically for Title I schools in under-resourced neighborhoods or communities. The schools that create caring communities typically have better test results and transformation for the community as a whole. As I started living each day more and more guided by the Spirit, I began to see the fruit being produced across so many different areas of my life.

An older principal in the district helped open my eyes to the role that we can have in our communities. I knew he was a Christian and also a board member of the men's rehab center in town. He called me up one day and asked me, "So how's your church?" I started telling him about the church I was going to in Aurora, but he interrupted me. "No, I mean, how is **your** church," meaning the teachers and students under my care in the district. I sort of laughed to myself and realized he was right. These are the people for whom I was responsible, walking with them through difficult moments of life and recognizing that God had a purpose and calling for each one of them. When we start to change the way we see people, everything changes.

SUMMARY

God's heart is a weaving together of all creation in justice, wholeness and delight, the Hebrew word *shalom*. And each of us has a role to play in this process of restoration, not just a task to do, but a fulfillment of who we are and what gives us purpose and joy. During this time God began to reconnect me to see this purpose in my job and day-to-day life, stirring that initial call to give Him my whole life.

REFLECTION

What gives you joy? If you were to "vision-cast," what three words come to mind?
Sometimes we feel like we are facing a huge, impenetrable brick wall, hopeless. Right now, what is your "brick wall?" Ask God to remind you of what your purpose and calling is in this time. Wait in silence and listening prayer, giving him space to bring it to mind. You may also ask him if there is anything that has distracted you or discouraged you from that original purpose. In my case, it wasn't a person or circumstance, but a belief that we hold that kept me back – for instance, my fear of being "unprofessional" or inappropriate.

ACTIVATION

Kirk Delaney invited anyone willing to receive dreams and visions from God to put out their hands. He prayed that they would receive seven nights of dreams. Are you willing to enter this request, ready to answer, "Speak Lord, for Your servant is listening."

[1] Cornelius Plantinga, Jr., *Not the Way It's Supposed to Be: A Breviary of Sin* (Grand Rapids: Eerdmans, 1995), 10, emphasis his.

Michael D Smith

CHAPTER 3: HOW TO HEAL SICK PEOPLE

Don't be afraid to take a big step. You can't cross a chasm in two small jumps.

— David Lloyd George

One thing I've noticed in my years in ministry in various churches is that many of us have developed a strange theology when it comes to healing. Some groups don't see it as part of something Jesus calls us to do today. Other people believe God can do it, but not that He would use us to do it. Still others might think God could use them to heal a headache, or back pain, but not something big like healing a blind person or making a crippled person walk.

The two-fold truth is very simple. Healing is impossible for us. Healing is easy for Jesus. There are no "little" or "big" miracles. As a brand-new twenty-year-old Christian in Mexico, I did not have a great level of faith or any training, but I prayed for a completely deaf woman and saw her instantly healed. More recently I had a funny experience praying for a blind man in church. We were in the front of a large church and I had him turn around and face the back of the sanctuary where there was a huge digital clock with neon numbers set up for speakers. I figured it would be a good thing to test his vision if it came in gradually. This seems to happen in Mark 8, and I think I was imagining a slow, gradual process like what happens when the eye doctor tests your vision. I prayed for the man once, and he looked up at the numbers on the clock I had mentioned, rubbed his eyes and looked again. Then he looked at me and took off running out the door. I guess he was healed instantly, and I am not sure which of us was more surprised at that moment. Other times I've seen God use me to heal people of back pain or a headache during my workday. As simple as it sounds, I've seen God use those little moments to have a huge effect.

In the beginning of this book I shared a story about the first time I took a step of faith and out of the blue prayed for a teacher at my school who was feeling sick, and within twenty minutes she was well again. Sometimes a healing moment can feel almost so simple that you could dismiss it, but the prayers of God bear fruit. As I look back over my treasure trove of miracle stories and transformed lives, I am amazed how many of them I can trace back to that first step of faith that I took, and the doors that were opened because of it. A few months after that prayer, I was walking in the hall when I saw this teacher and her teacher assistant walking together, and her assistant was crying. As they approached me, the teacher who had been healed turned to the woman and said, "You need to pray with Mr. Smith. He has something special."

That teacher had begun sending her worst problem students to me and expecting a miracle to happen. There was a severely hyperactive boy in her class, and the teacher told the mother to make an appointment with me to get prayer! At 11 a.m. the mother came in with our parent liaison to translate. She told me she had been told to come pray with me. I think she thought it was a form of punishment for her, since her kid was acting up in class. When I asked her what she wanted prayer for, she started telling me things I think she thought were the "right" answer: "That I can be involved in the school more, come to parent teacher conferences, read to my kids more...."

With a wink to the Holy Spirit I nodded and smiled, "Okay, let's just pray." As we started to pray, I began getting tingling in my upper back, so I asked her if she had pain in that spot.

She said, "Yes," and I asked her to check her pain levels, because she was about to witness a miracle. She had been in severe pain, but her level went from a ten to a zero in just one prayer. She looked at me in shock and showed me that her arms were covered in goosebumps. That day in my office she accepted Jesus. I gave their family a Bible and connected them to the local Catholic parish, Our Lady of Good Counsel. After that, something seemed to have shifted for that family and we no longer had any behavior issues with her kids in our classes. That kind of healing happened through a sympathy pain. A sympathy pain is an unusual and out-of-the-blue pain that suddenly manifests in our body. The best way I would describe it is God trying to quickly get my attention to pray for a healing miracle. When a sympathy pain shows up that matches pain they're having in their body, I know a miracle is about to happen.

Ever since I became a Christian, it's been obvious to me that healing was something that could only come from God, and was just as real as believing in God himself. For years I went to a church that didn't talk about it or practice it at all, but once I began hearing it preached and taught as regularly as it appears in the gospels, it became a natural part of my lifestyle. Almost every day I encounter people who are sick or have some pain, and almost every day, or at least every other day, I see God heal people.

It actually became so normal at my school that my secretaries would have to regularly buzz in families coming from other schools to get prayer and set up appointments with me. When you start praying for people on a regular basis, God heals them, and word gets out. People in the community would come in off the streets asking for prayer.

I've shared a few healing stories already in this book, and I want to look at a passage of Scripture to use as a helpful guide for understanding some of the dynamics of healing, and to help correct some of the bad theology that can get in the way of God using us to heal the sick on a daily basis. In John 9:1-5 (NLT), Jesus heals a man who had been born blind since birth.

> As Jesus was walking along, he saw a man who had been blind from birth. "Rabbi," his disciples asked him, "why was this

man born blind? Was it because of his own sins or his parents' sins?"

"It was not because of his sins or his parents' sins," Jesus answered. "This happened so the power of God could be seen in him. We must quickly carry out the tasks assigned us by the one who sent us."

Christians often fall into two theological camps. At one extreme, some groups may be tempted to assume that the fault of not getting healed is in the sick person. People have sometimes felt blamed for just not having "enough faith." At another extreme, some traditions tend to see sickness as the sovereign will of God, or a kind of blessing from God used to build character. It's true that while God can use bad things (and all things) for the good of those that love Him, it is clear from this passage that the "works of God" and the work of Jesus in this world, is healing. If you assume that everything that exists is the sovereign work of God, then you must assume that God wants a lot of sickness, disease, oppression, and bad things in the world. Yet Jesus came to do the work of God, and He healed all their diseases. My basic principle is "Keep Imitating Jesus." Keep praying for the sick, keep casting out oppression from people's lives, keep assuming that if Jesus were here, the person in front of you would be completely healed. This is the work of God we see represented in the Bible. As we go about the Father's business, He will show up in unexpected and amazing ways.

As I began growing in the confidence to declare healing and speak these things into being, it seemed like they literally started happening. At our church, I had heard many sermons preached along those lines, but as I stepped up and started to do the things, I really saw it to be true. I believe that most of us have far more authority than we are currently using. Sometimes it even seems that God is the one waiting on us, not the other way around. I've found that even when it seems like nothing is happening, I will often see later that the entire situation has been reversed. Just because it doesn't happen in the moment, doesn't mean it's not going to happen.

> *After saying this, He spit on the ground, made some mud with the saliva, and put it on the man's eyes. "Go," He told him, "wash in the Pool of Siloam" (this word means "Sent"). So the man went and washed, and came home seeing.*
> John 9:6-7 (NIV)

In Scripture we sometimes see Jesus doing something tangible when He heals people. Someday I'd like to ask Jesus why He sometimes used spit to heal people's eyes. That's not something I would recommend trying to do, but I do often have people do something that engages them with the process. In the Bible when lame people are healed, they are told to stand and walk. Usually when I pray for back pain or shoulder pain, I will have the person try to bend, or twist, and test it out. Sometimes it seems like nothing at all has happened, but as soon as they test it out it seems like suddenly the healing takes place. I wouldn't be surprised in the Bible when the lame are healed, if their healing actually happens as they start to stand to the ground, not before.

One year, while attending a healing conference, I prayed for a woman with fibromyalgia. At the time, I didn't even know what it was. The woman explained to me that it's a nervous system disorder that amplifies sensations of pain all over the body. She unzipped her tall black boots and showed me large welts all over her legs. She said it hurt so bad it in that moment it felt like razors were cutting through her skin. I remember we had to pray multiple times. The first time we prayed she felt a little better, but could still feel the burning pain. I had her test out her legs to notice any differences specifically. She said on a level of pain it had gone down from a ten (where we started) to an eight. We prayed several more times, each time the pain diminishing until she looked with astonishment at her legs and noticed that the welts had gone down and were hardly noticeable. She was so excited she asked to pray again, and this time she noticed tingling all over legs. Her pain was at a zero and when she looked down she saw that the bumps were completely gone. At this point I asked her if she could test it out, and try to do something that she normally could never do. She had very long fingernails and she scratched her legs all the way down with her nails in amazement saying, "I haven't been able to do this for years!" She received a complete healing and a doctor's concurrence later. At that point, I asked her to pray with me for another woman who needed healing, and she was healed as well.

It can feel daunting to pray for healing, and I think breaking it down in a practical way can make it concrete and also make it more encouraging. When you first start out, you might feel tempted to go for the "all or nothing" approach because it feels a little easier. Sometimes if you pray for someone and ask them if they are healed, they will say, "No," where in actuality the pain may have gone from a level ten to a level one. If they still feel a little twinge they will say, "No." This discourages you, and discourages them. Since Jesus once prayed for a blind man in two stages, I figure we have permission to pray for someone at least six or seven times to see them healed. My advice is to be specific about the healing that needs to happen, be patient with the process, and be observant. Sometimes the pain might not go away right away, but the person may begin to experience heat in their body or tingling sensations.

Some people have said it feels like electricity going through their body, or some people have felt nothing at all, then come back two days later and report that a huge cyst the size of a grapefruit is completely gone from their body. Remember, your faith doesn't depend on their reaction or lack of reaction, it depends on Jesus. Be confident, be practical, take your time. I would say 80% of the time that I pray with someone, I see an immediate change or decrease in pain. If absolutely nothing happens at all, sometimes that's the first clue that this is not simply a physical ailment, but a spiritual infirmity. Without freaking the person out, I simply pray against a spirit of infirmity, and bind any unclean spirit or generational oppression, as I sense the Spirit leading. Many times that leads to a breakthrough in physical healing. Occasionally the person reaches a level one or two with the pain, and if we've already prayed several times, I will tell them to keep praying it out over the week. Often I hear reports that they were completely healed the next day or within the next few days.

> *So the man went and washed, and came home seeing. His neighbors and those who had formerly seen him begging asked, "Isn't this the same man who used to sit and beg?"*

Michael D Smith

John 9:7b-8 (NLT)

When someone is healed, I always share Christ with them if they haven't received Him in their hearts, and I often invite them to then pray for someone else who needs healing. In this Scripture passage the name of the pool was called, "Sent." I believe that when you receive a healing miracle in your life, you become a living testimony to release that healing to other people. I have seen many powerful miracles occur this way, even by people who were not even technically "believers." God used them to heal others. The enemy would like to steal this seed of faith immediately, and I often find that sharing with others what God has done often helps solidify the testimony of faith in their hearts.

For us, I think the important thing is to resolve in your heart that you will continue to do this out of simple obedience to Christ, without getting so bothered or fixated on the results. As you "sow" generously, taking the time to stop and to pray for all the sick that come your way, you will definitely start to see miracles and healings result. Just keep praying and don't give up or get discouraged. Of course, in the beginning you may be expecting nothing to happen, and maybe it seems like it doesn't, but sooner than you could imagine is possible, healing will become so "normal" that you become surprised and confused when people aren't healed. As I grew in the Spirit, learning about healing and how this is available to us, there came a point when I realized, "I am going to have to overcome this complacency to just mind my own business and do my own thing. Now that I know this is real, and God can do these things on a daily basis, how can I keep this stuff secret?"

For me, with my personality, I had to pray and ask the Holy Spirit to make it obvious to me when it was a Holy Spirit moment. In many ways I am a typical administrator. Sometimes I'm directly involved with situations at my school, but more often than not my role is behind-the-scenes. I work with deadlines, being on task, planning things out, and sticking to my routine without rocking the boat— that's the way my personality is built and it's made me successful at my job. Sometimes I've feared that it's made it difficult for me to follow what the Spirit is doing in the moment, especially when it involves breaking social norms and unspoken codes of conduct that reinforce what "normal" interactions look like. Those things were often uncomfortable for me, and kept me in my own routine for years. Since I am a routine-oriented person, I try to create new routines that invite the Holy Spirit to "interrupt" me, intentionally invite God into my life and into situations. Creating those consistent habits throughout my day allows Him to train me to grow in sensitivity to what He is doing. If we ask Him, He will provide us with opportunities, and as we are faithful to obey we will start to see those kinds of things happen more and more.

Remember, if you have a job you work at, a neighborhood you live in, a grocery store you shop at — You already have a mission field, a calling, and a purpose. You don't have to make something up. God is already at work in the lives of people around us; we get to jump in and join Him. Ask God to open your eyes to see that the fields are white for the harvest. My daily practice of walking the building every hour to pray is a good example of this, and actually makes me really good at my job as principal. My prayer list is another example of that, along with my daily prayer for God to "highlight" people and situations that He wants me to step into. With practice, I now have become aware of how God does that. Sometimes it feels like certain people and situations sort of pop out visually, almost like they have an extra lamp shining on them. It's just a subtle thing I've noticed over the years that God does to help me, and when I see that cue from Him, it reminds me to drop everything and obey. Usually God does something good.

I had originally been inspired by my pastor to try to be available for God to use me at my work, in my place of influence. For me, I finally realized it became a lifestyle when I started doing things outside of my job and outside of my church. One year we took a road trip as a family to New Hampshire, and rented a hotel on Hampton Beach. There I was, eating breakfast at the hotel, when all of a sudden my arm started twinging, like a strong tickle on my left forearm. In my spirit I sensed God quickly tell me, "It's not YOUR arm; it's for the breakfast attendant." I got excited now, because I realized God was speaking to me for someone in the room, and I was confident I was about to see someone healed. I looked around the room and noticed one of the breakfast workers seemed to really stand out to me. I could describe it almost like a glow, though
he wasn't literally glowing; it was almost like an overlay that made him pop out to me.

I waited until the other guests had cleared out and he had a little break in his job, then I asked if everything was all right with him, or if he had some pain in his left arm. He told me that actually he had ripped up his shoulder a few years ago and he has experienced pain in that arm ever since. As simple as possible, I told him, "Sometimes I pray for people and God heals them. Do you think God could heal your arm?"

The worker looked at me confused, "Who? Did you say 'God'?" He paused then nodded his head, "I guess so, yes." I prayed for him and the pain left. He said he wasn't sure he was healed because the pain did come and go, but still he was surprised that suddenly his arm actually felt good.

For me that moment was a turning point. Instead of trying to force myself to be more intentional at work and the people I was "supposed" to be taking care of, praying for healing and expecting God to intervene at any time became a part of who I was, something I began doing anywhere I found myself, whether on vacation or at the grocery store or at one of my kids' events. I would regularly pray, "Lord, what are you doing here?"

As I began to do this on a daily basis, in the work setting, I would say that almost without fail there would be a change or an improvement. Occasionally in this book you will hear me share stories when I felt led to pray for a long time with someone, often involving not just physical healing but something connected to their past or emotional wounds. Normally on a day-to-day basis, I would say that 95% of the time I pray for less than two minutes and have them check it out. I have found that if a person has been highlighted to me by the Holy Spirit, there is almost always a change, 20-50% better. I usually pray with someone until the problem goes down to a two, and then I trust that it will get better. It seems like 80% of the time healing happens in front of my eyes,

20% of the time it's hard to tell, or it seems like nothing has happened. When a person has not been highlighted, the percentages of seeing healing on the spot go way down. If I pray with someone twice and there is absolutely no change in the level of pain, then I usually do a prayer breaking off infirmity or curses. At that point I will usually see some change start to happen; people will feel a change. After that, I usually drop it and move on. Holy Spirit will usually give another opportunity if needed.

Because I was already a very busy person, I am always trying to be pretty efficient, looking for ways to multitask. While I am driving around town or if I have a day of running errands, I have stopped listening to music on the radio, and instead use the time to pray and ask God to keep me sensitive to what He is doing. In that way I am staying "on mission" more and more in my life. When I first show up to places I try to check in with the Holy Spirit, "What are You doing in this place and what's my part in it?" From the outside, you wouldn't notice anything unusual about what I am doing or the way I am behaving, but by being intentional like that, it seems like everywhere I go stuff starts to happen. God opens up doors and I get more opportunities. I believe this is true for all of us, in whatever walk of life you are in. As you stay connected to God, you will start to see little moments of "heavenly" intervention happening all around you. Most, if not all, of the time that people have been healed, they receive Christ. I had a talk about this with Damien Stayne, a Catholic evangelist out of London. We had been ministering together in a conference in Poland, and he heard me tell several testimonies of healing. He looked at me for a few minutes and then asked, "What is the percentage of a situation when someone has gotten healed, and then you present the gospel?" After thinking about it for a few minutes, I had to admit that it was every time. "I think it's 99.9%. Anytime that someone has been healed, I ask something about a relationship with God, and in those situations, I can only think of one person who said no. In other situations where the person didn't get healed, and didn't want a relationship with Jesus, I simply have to trust that their spiritual journey is not over yet, and as we faithfully witness, the Holy Spirit will continue to guide their lives and follow up. For us, nothing changes. We faithfully pray for the sick and share a message of God's love and forgiveness for sins everywhere we go. It's not about the results, it's about our obedience to Christ, and we simply play our part. The real victory belongs to him and is accomplished by him, it doesn't depend on our performance.

> *Some of the Pharisees said, "This man is not from God, for he does not keep the Sabbath." But others asked, "How can a sinner perform such signs?" So they were divided.*
> John 9:16 (NIV)

One thing that sometimes holds people back mentally is the fear that they are not "good enough" or "advanced enough" Christians to perform a miracle. In the Catholic tradition, people who do miracles are the "saints," and the idea is that these are almost perfect superheroes of the Christian faith. In the Bible, we see Jesus sending out the seventy to do miracles before they could even technically be considered Christians, before they believed Jesus was the Son of God, and before they received the Holy Spirit. In the Bible, the disciples even complain that people who were not Christ-followers were able to perform miracles in the name of Jesus. In Mark 9:38-40 (NIV), Jesus acknowledges these miracles and tells him, "'Do not stop him,' Jesus said. 'For no one who does a miracle in my name can in the next moment say anything bad about me, for whoever is not against us is for us.'" If even unbelievers can perform miracles in the name of Jesus, that sets the bar pretty low for what it takes to perform miracles, but at the same time it should set us free from the fear that "miracles" depend on our own righteousness or our own level of holiness. I like the way one of my mentors used to put it, "God loves THEM so much, He is even willing to use ME to reach them." It's not about us. Healing and salvation and transformed lives are not about who we are, but about who Jesus is, and the love of God for His lost sons and daughters. Of course, our goal is that everything we do comes from relationship with Jesus and is guided by the Holy Spirit working in our hearts.

Sometimes it can feel like humility to assume that God would probably never be able to use someone like us – with our sins, weaknesses, and character issues – to heal someone else. But beware that even though it appears humble, this kind of theology can be rooted in a religious mindset or a religious spirit. The grace of God in our lives makes it possible for us to follow Jesus in every area of our life, and to simply do the things Jesus did as an ordinary man on this earth. He encountered the same ridicule any one of us might imagine facing, "Who do you think you are, that you can heal people?" In fact, if you begin to pray for people and see healings and miracles happen on a regular basis, you might be surprised to find out who the people are that oppose you the most. More often than not, it's not unbelievers, but believers who are offended, judgmental, and critical:

LEAP

> *Then they turned again to the blind man, "What have you to say about him? It was your eyes he opened."... "Nobody has ever heard of opening the eyes of a man born blind. If this man were not from God, he could do nothing," he said. To this they replied, "You were steeped in sin at birth; how dare you lecture us!" And they threw him*
> John 9:17, 32-34 (NIV)

Whether or not someone is healed, you will often face some form of accusation. When miracles and healings start to happen, opposition often follows and the enemy begins to manifest his anger. With every kind of persecution or criticism you may face, you have a decision. On one hand it will be tempting to become hurt and upset with the way people may treat you. Many Christians who are doing wonderful ministries end up falling for the trap of becoming hurt and bitter because of that treatment, and the results of how they are talked about, misunderstood, and friendships they may lose in the process, even close family members.

On the other hand, I have also met many Christians who prayed for a godly family member, a beloved friend, and not seen them healed. The enemy will often whisper lies of bitterness telling them that healing doesn't "work," that God is not fair, or they are not loved. Watching a loved one battle a debilitating sickness is a terribly painful experience and often beyond our ability to comprehend.

In my school, I watched as a sweet six-year-old battled leukemia. I was very close with him and his family and had known him since preschool when he was first diagnosed. He was frail and had lost his hair during chemo sessions. His mother was active in the community and really liked me. He had been slowly recovering, but then the leukemia came back worse than ever. He was going back into the hospital for chemo treatments again and his mother had asked me for tutoring. I told her I believed in the power of prayer and asked if it would be okay if I prayed for him. She agreed and told me to pray for him as much as I could, even pull him out of classes to pray for him during the day. Whenever I thought about it, I would have an assistant bring him up in a wheelchair and keep him in my office working, and I would pray for him as he worked. We had a lot of happy memories in those days, and I really got to care about him. Over time he became weaker, and in October of that year he was taken to Chicago Children's hospital intensive care unit, where he was dying. When we heard he was very sick, my pastor and I drove into Chicago to pray with him. The next day he suddenly recovered and was discharged, even well enough to come back to school. We were all overjoyed. The next time he was getting sick again, I called him up to my office and asked him if he wanted to pray for healing like we did before in the hospital.

"Do you want prayer to get healed?"

He said, "No." He added, "I want to pray because I've had dreams that my brother hated me." I agreed to pray with him and as we prayed, I invited the Holy Spirit to come. There was a strong presence of God in the room and he began crying. I asked him if he wanted a relationship with Jesus, and told him that Jesus loved him and loved his brother. He accepted Jesus into his heart in

March. In May he had his kindergarten graduation, and the next day he died.

That was one of the toughest times for me as principal. I held a memorial prayer service for him, announcing, "Nobody is bound to be here, but we will be praying and anyone is welcome to join us." Not one staff member missed it. You see God heal, but then you realize that when you don't see healing, it's part of the natural law at work in the world. We don't always understand. My premise is to keep moving forward. Time and time again I have seen prayer make a difference. Not everything will make sense now, and we don't have all the answers, but I trust that one day it will be clear. I am encouraged by the following verses that concludes that passage:

> *Jesus heard that they had thrown him out, and when He found him, He said, "Do you believe in the Son of Man?"*
> *"Who is he, sir?" the man asked. "Tell me so that I may believe in him."*
> *Jesus said, "You have now seen Him; in fact, He is the one speaking with you."*
> *Then the man said, "Lord, I believe," and he worshiped Him.*
> John 9:35-38 (NLT)

All of us will face situations in life that make us feel abandoned, outcast, and maybe even far from God's presence. Whether it's caused by the treatment of people around us or by a circumstance in our life that made us feel confused and unloved by God. When we are in that place, Jesus comes to find us and to love us. There is no circumstance or rejection or pain that places us outside of His ability to meet us or for us to meet Him in a new way. I may never know the answer of why this young boy eventually lost his life to cancer, but I do know that through prayer, he and his family and many of my staff encountered the tangible love of God. I know that he met Jesus and realized that he needed His greater love in his young life. With all of his understanding and heart, he embraced Jesus' message of love and forgiveness, before going to meet Him in heaven.

We are not in charge of the outcome, God is. We simply have a choice each day how to spend our time and resources to trust God with our obedience. For me, and for many of us, it's something that naturally ebbs and flows all the time. We each go through different seasons in life, and for me I just try to be intentional about not letting those moments go by, but trusting that God can meet me in whatever season I'm in. When I think it's over, or I've lost the way, it's never over.

SUMMARY
As we go about the Father's business, He will show up in unexpected and amazing ways. The important thing is to resolve in your heart that you will continue to pray for healing out of simple obedience to Christ, without getting so bothered or fixated on the results. It's not about us.... healing, and salvation, and transformed lives is not about who we are, but about who Jesus is, and the love of God for His lost sons and daughters.

REFLECTION
Jesus noticed as He walked through life, He was aware. He saw Zacchaeus in the tree and Bartimaeus by the side of the road. Do

you move through your day open to God's leading and prodding? Try to create new routines that invite the Holy Spirit to "interrupt" your day, intentionally invite God into your life and into situations. When I first show up to places I try to check in with the Holy Spirit, "What are You doing in this place and what's my part in it?"

ACTIVATION
Tips for Ministering Healing
- o Check what it feels like before you begin.
- o Set expectations that you are about to witness a miracle. (that throws people off)
- o Expect now.
- o Is this symptom a red herring? Or is it the root of the issue?
- o When the Holy Spirit tells me something that is hidden or dark, we speak life and dig for gold and emphasize the person's true identity.
- o Pause and ask the Holy Spirit, "What is going on here? What will make a difference?" (Look for signs, look for moving of the Holy Spirit. Ask them if they feel anything.)

Michael D Smith

CHAPTER 4: MIRACLES IN A CRISIS

The Chinese use two brush strokes to write the word 'crisis.' One brush stroke stands for danger; the other for opportunity. In a crisis, be aware of the danger--but recognize the opportunity. — John F. Kennedy

If you ask most churchgoers what is the "perfect Christian life," many people might describe a cross between Martha Stewart and the American Dream. As much as we'd all love every day to go smoothly, our jobs to flourish, people to love us, our kids to do great, our marriages to be perfect — the reality of the kingdom of God we see in the gospels is often full of problems, messy, and far from the average ideal of "perfect." Although Jesus pleased God in every way, it should encourage us that He lived out His ministry surrounded by difficulties and dysfunction.

Have you ever noticed that many of Jesus' miracles happened because of a crisis? He was at a party and the drinks ran out — it was this crisis that led His first disciples to put their faith in Him. Maybe a divine beer run is not the place where you'd expect God to begin His work on earth in human form, but it's certainly relatable. From there, the level of crisis scales up pretty quickly. Another time He was sleeping in a boat and all of a sudden a terrible storm arose. Some of his famous miracles happened when He became repeatedly stranded in the desert with thousands of people needing food. People in crisis swarmed to Him, from paralytics, to lepers, to the blind and bleeding. He and his followers were often broke, being constantly threatened and harassed by religious and secular authorities and even close friends and family members. From reading the Bible, it looks like a day in the life of Jesus was a day full of problems. In the Bible he is described as "a man acquainted with sorrows." When He was going to visit His friend and His friend got sick and died, Jesus wept openly. We are warned that in this life we will encounter hardships and suffering of every kind. Don't be discouraged.

In Jesus we see a man who is deeply compassionate, full of emotion, and acutely sensitive to the thoughts and feelings of people around Him. In Scripture we see that He gets hungry, thirsty, tired, angry, and sad. One of the things that sets Jesus apart is that He does not seem to be afflicted with anxiety and stress. He seems to be confident about God's timing, His provision, and His miraculous solution to any situation. He even seems appalled when people give up faith that God will do something. In each circumstance, Jesus releases a provision from heaven with a wide range of sources and often surprising solutions. Sometimes He used mud, a random fish in the ocean, a simple walk over the water, somebody's lunch, or a nearby fig tree to demonstrate the reality of the kingdom.

One of the things about starting to live life by the Holy Spirit, is that when problems would rise up in my workplace or daily life, instead of panicking, I began to realize that each of these situations was actually an opportunity for God to do something cool. As I grew in awareness of God's presence with me, I became more confident that He actually gives us authority to release blessings of heaven in every situation.

One day I saw one of my teachers from Spain, a team leader at my school, walking in the hall looking frazzled and stressed. I asked her what was wrong, and she confessed that she had misplaced an extremely important folder of information that was supposed to be turned in. She had been working on the data folders that I had given the teachers to fill out, and she couldn't find the stack of data she had painstakingly collected from all the teachers. I asked her if everyone else had their things; they did, but she couldn't find hers anywhere. She told me she had just spent over an hour searching every single part of her classroom and desk and they were not to be found anywhere. I said, "Let's pray for them to appear right now."

We prayed together for the documents to surface. Then I told her, "Go look quickly in all the same places that you just looked and come show them to me when you find them." Ten minutes later, she stood in front of my desk holding the folder of lost files, with a stunned look on her face.

"It's impossible. I walked in my classroom and opened my desk and they were sitting right there on top in the first drawer. I searched that same drawer three times before this, and they definitely were not there."

I had to smile. I just love watching to see what Jesus does in these situations when we put our faith in Him. I told her, "Jesus put them there to let you know that He loves you. You just witnessed a miracle and I want you to tell your family in Spain what just happened." I had several similar incidents with that teacher, and it created an expectation that circumstances were under God's control.

I saw her walking down the hall with one of her assistants, who was crying. She told her assistant, "You need to pray with Mr. Smith." I agreed to pray with her, "Yeah, come to my office in five minutes." A little bit later she came into my office and shared about the issues she was going through and we prayed. I told her that Jesus loved her and wanted a relationship with her. I asked if she wanted Jesus in her heart and she said yes. I took her down to the Spirit-filled teacher to follow up with her. I knew that she was caring enough and patient enough to follow up with her and walk with her on the journey.

Twenty minutes later the same TA knocked on my door again, this time asking if I would pray with her son. I didn't quite understand what was going on, until half an hour later when her adult son showed up at the school. He had just been fired from the bank because $15,000 was missing and they said it was him. I asked if he did it, and he said no. I knew the family was an honorable family, and I believed him. We prayed for supernatural restitution and whoever was behind it would immediately be brought to light and justice. I asked if he wanted to ask Jesus into his life and he said yes. He had been brought up Catholic and so I asked him to speak to Father Dave, and tell him that we had prayed together. A few days later the TA came to tell me the good news that when they did an investigation, it was proven that her son's supervisor had stolen the money and tried to pin it on her son. The supervisor was fired and her son got his job back.

God became flesh. As Christians, we believe Jesus is the manifestation of God's love walking on earth. Everything belongs to Him, and He is above every situation and circumstance. While He walked on earth, He was interruptible. People would stop Him and ask Him for the things that mattered to them, and He responded. Sometimes I think we have an idea that God is so far away in heaven, far too busy to take care of the situations we face each day. Jesus shows otherwise. Sometimes we mistake the idea of God's sovereignty to believe that every single thing that happens is the predestined will of God. Jesus shows otherwise. On a daily basis, people ask Him to intervene and He did. They asked Him for help, and He acted. He didn't seem confused wondering what was the will of God. He walked on the earth with compassion and confidence, and I believe we can do the same.

> *On the third day a wedding took place at Cana in Galilee. Jesus' mother was there, and Jesus and his disciples had also been invited to the wedding. When the wine was gone, Jesus' mother said to him, "They have no more wine,"*
> John 2:1-3 (NIV)

Like Mary, we can continually present every situation to God. We do not need to get busy creating our own solutions or stressing out, when the truth is we have access to Jesus at all times. There are so many situations and I believe Jesus has a creative resolution for each one. When Jesus invites us to go into all the world and preach the good news, I believe there's a built-in promise that He wants to reveal the goodness of the Father. We do not need to be afraid of letting people down. Instead we can be confident, like Mary, who seems to presume upon the goodness of God. I imagine a twinkle in the eye of Jesus, as He and his mother are having this conversation:

> *"Woman, why do you involve me?" Jesus replied. "My hour has not yet come."*
> *His mother said to the servants, "Do whatever He tells you,"*
> John 2:4-5 (NIV)

The next part of this passage shows what is often the hard part for us to follow. Many of us may ask God for something, many of us will turn to him in private with our requests and hope he does a miracle. With trust and love Mary comes to Jesus, and I believe the miracle lies in her faith to do whatever He asks.

> *Standing nearby were six stone water jars, used for Jewish ceremonial washing. Each could hold twenty to thirty gallons. Jesus told the servants, "Fill the jars with water." When the jars had been filled, He said, "Now dip some out, and take it to the master of ceremonies." So the servants followed His instructions*
> John 2:6-8 (NLT)

At this point the servants are on the spot. They must take water from the cleaning supplies, and offer it to the most important man at the banquet. Would he mock them? Would he embarrass them? Would he hurl the water in their face? What Jesus was asking was completely against the norm. The master of the banquet would have been the most important person present, their boss in a sense. Imagine the pressure they must have felt. A Jewish wedding would have been a reflection of status and prestige in the community, something the family would have taken months, maybe even years to plan and save up for. The servants were faced with a choice. They knew they had water in the jugs; they had just drawn it themselves. The Bible doesn't say that Jesus turned the water into fine wine, and then asked them to take it to him. So many times when I step out to pray for healing or face a crisis, I don't have any idea what is going to happen, but I believe that if I obey Jesus, something will happen. I wonder at what point in this story the water turned to wine? Did it turn to wine when they took the first step towards the master of ceremonies? Or maybe as they poured it into his glass?

Although I don't know the answer to this question, I believe there is often a powerful miracle that takes place as we step into obedience, and put the weight of trust into the moment. The book of Hebrews describes faith as the "confidence" in what we hope for, the "assurance" of things not seen. Some versions use the word "substance."

When praying for healing, I like to take the time to put some weight into the moment, often asking people to test it out in some way if they can. Although there may not be any flash of light, or it seems like nothing has happened, as they test it out, suddenly they find that all the pain is gone, or the full range of motion is restored. I believe many times the actual miracle occurs in the activation, as we take confidence in what we are doing and the promise that God has given us.

> *When the master of ceremonies tasted the water that was now wine, not knowing where it had come from (though, of course, the servants knew)....*
> John 2:9 (NLT)

Nobody realized, except the servants. With Jesus' miracles, they are often so subtle and so sweet that you have to remind yourself of what just happened. Jesus could have had wine from heaven pour out of the ceiling, or start to manifest from the empty goblets. When he feeds the five thousand he could have rained down manna from heaven as God did in the past. What I've noticed in the ministry of Jesus on earth is that he often chooses the simple ordinary things of life: a little boy's lunch, the cleaning pots that would have been found in any Jewish home, a fisherman's net, and a poor girl about to be married — to manifest the power of heaven. In the same way, we don't have to look for extraordinary circumstances to see God at work. He compares our faith to a mustard seed, or to yeast. The plain, everyday ingredients of normal life, when combined with trust and obedience, can display the power of heaven. As you offer him the simple everyday moments of need that you encounter, and step forward in a faith of obedience, I believe you will see miracles happen. The beautiful thing about inviting Jesus into these everyday situations and problems of life is that you get to know

Him more. Jesus is so much more creative, gracious, and kind than we could ever imagine, and He loves to reveal His heart for people in surprising ways.

> ...he called the bridegroom over. "A host always serves the best wine first," he said. "Then, when everyone has had a lot to drink, he brings out the less expensive wine. But you have kept the best until now!" This miraculous sign at Cana in Galilee was the first time Jesus revealed His glory. And His disciples believed in Him.
>
> John 2:10-11 (NLT)

Many times as I've stepped out in faith, I've seen God not only solve the "problem," but provide a solution that was so much more wonderful than the initial problem was bad. Prayer is definitely not a magic formula that produces the same results every time, but it's a connection from heaven, through us. Where we walk, Jesus walks, because He lives inside of us. His goodness far exceeds the weight of any problem we face, and that is an important thing to keep in mind as you step out in prayer for the first time, or for the four hundredth time. We are called to reveal His glory, and as we pray for people, we get to watch and see what God will do.

I know many of us face heartbreaking circumstances that may leave us feeling helpless. What can you say to a parent that loses a child? A friend whose business goes bankrupt? Some situations seem final, yet God in His mercy is able to bring about good.

LEAP

One year I was heartbroken to hear of the hardship one of my sweetest and most dependable teachers was undergoing. Her husband was leaving her, and she had a houseful of kids at home. One of the kids was severely autistic, in a wheelchair. During a pre-observation convergence, she ended up sharing with me about how difficult it was for her other son and daughter feeling left out because so much attention was spent on her nonverbal son. She was losing her housing situation, couldn't keep up with the monthly payments and was really in a desperate place without enough money to provide for the family. I reached for my wallet, and she told me, "Mike, I'm not asking for money, please just pray." We prayed together for God's provision for her family, and for the plans He had for her life. Though everything seemed destroyed, we trusted the situation to God.

The very next morning, she came to my office with her eyes sparkling and told me that she had a visitor to her home the previous afternoon. A Nigerian refugee, dressed with headdress and full Nigerian clothes, mysteriously came to her front door and knocked, and asked her if she could use some extra food. She dropped off four boxes of food for her. The next few months money kept amazingly coming out of the woodwork to pay the rent. Even though it was far out of her budget, she managed to keep the house, and by the end of the year she actually met and married a kind businessman from a church she was attending and they moved into their own home together. He also had children of his own, and they combined families. She and her new husband invited my wife and me over to celebrate.

I think one of the things I noticed was that as I stepped out boldly offering prayer in desperate situations, people began to come to me when there was a crisis or a time of need in their life. Even people who normally would not feel comfortable sharing personal hardships or illnesses they were suffering, felt comfortable to come to me for prayer when they really had nowhere else to turn. God loves it when we turn to Him at any time in our lives. What amazed me as well, is that in her case, He actually used some of the poorest and most unlikely people in our community to provide for this woman's needs. Sometimes we look to people in our community who we think have the resources to provide a solution, but actually God is able to raise up His answer to our prayer from the most unlikely people in our life.

This was an example of how after simply making that decision to take more radical steps in my work life, praying for people in person, and doing prayer walks in the school, I quickly began to notice a huge increase in the way God would use me. Once an hour I would get up from my office and do a sweep of the school where I could hit every corner of the building in one big loop. During that time of walking, I would pray peace and that the Holy Spirit would reveal hidden things. As I opened myself up to be available to God, it seemed that without fail He would use this prayer walk time to manifest His presence in our school, perform miracles, and often give me strategic opportunities to prevent bad things from happening. One time I was sitting at my desk working and I got the urge, "I need to drop what I'm doing and go on a prayer walk." I opened the door to the boys' bathroom and there was a kid with a lighter trying to light the trash on fire. If I had been there two minutes later, it would have been a completely different situation.

Many times I was faced with a crisis that exploded right in front of my desk. People would come into my office all the time who were furious, full of rage or anger. In those moments I would stop and ask, "Holy Spirit, what's going on here?" In those times of crisis, He would often give me wisdom and show me what the real issue was. In our natural self, we might be tempted to defend ourselves or take it personally, but the Holy Spirit would usually show me that it's not about me, and guide me with a question or a solution that would completely transform the situation. I ask the Holy Spirit very specific questions, like "Why am I here? What is my role in this situation? Why is this happening?"

One of my teachers had a family crisis when her father was dying. In the past I might have told her I'd pray for her, but this time when she asked me to pray for her father, I actually took the initiative to go to her home after work hours on a Friday night and pray for him in person. He was an older guy in his 90s. His eyes had swollen terribly. One had popped and was missing, and the other eye was blind. The father also had high blood pressure, high blood sugar, and he was completely depressed because his wife had just died. I walked into the apartment where he was lying on the bed. This was something new for me. His daughters politely let me in and then stood at the back, motioning me forward to pray.

I prayed against depression, restoration of sight, and regeneration of his eye. I prayed two or three times, until I noticed he was snoring. I looked at the girls, and they shrugged. "We are done," I said, and left. It might have seemed like an awkward moment, or that nothing had happened.

Monday we went back to school, and the teacher told me that Saturday morning her father had jumped up out of bed and stayed up all day chatting. He was totally normal. He wanted to look for me and thank me. He told them that he understood everything I said, even though I had been praying in English and he was only a Spanish speaker. He said he wanted me to come over and pray with him again. He didn't feel any depression anymore.

Sometimes I believe that the part of their spirit that wants to be free and wants to be healed can recognize the Holy Spirit in you, even without knowing why. Many times people I don't even know will come in and tell me all their problems. When I find myself in that situation I have to stop and recognize, "Wait a minute, this is a special moment. God how do You want me to respond?" Once I started to pray in my quiet time, asking God to make me aware of these things, He faithfully did. I believe as we become available, God is ready and willing to use us, even in the most unlikely circumstances. I have seen God use me to reach people who didn't even speak the same language as me. One time I was sharing a story of what God did, and a Korean relative was standing there who didn't speak English. He heard me sharing what Jesus did in healing a man. Even though he didn't understand what I was saying, his relative told him I was speaking about Jesus, and he said he felt something in his heart, and he wanted Jesus. He left that week for Korea, having given his life to Jesus. I believe as we step out in obedience, our life becomes a message of good news that people can feel and respond to, even without words.

I started the practice of keeping a "hotlist" sheet of paper tucked into my Bible, where I would write the names of any students or situations that seemed to be in particular crisis. There were usually five or six items on that list, and as I saw God resolve one issue, I would add another. Over the years God faithfully transformed those situations before my eyes.

One of those crisis situations was an agonizing decision that most organizational leaders must face: having to fire people. A teacher at our school was an older woman who had come out of retirement to fill a vacancy. She was a friendly, well-liked teacher around campus that knew many of the students personally, calling them by their own personalized nickname. She always had a kind word or joke to share, and often knew just what to say to a seemingly unreachable student. She struggled with her health and energy levels. She would often fall asleep in class and we could see through the monitors the kids going out of control and beginning to destroy school property, or running through the building to disrupt other classes. It was something we would never have tolerated in any other teacher, yet she felt like family. I dreaded having to be the "bad guy" who fired her, especially when I knew she and her husband were going through a hard time and probably needed the extra income. She was having health problems and I knew she was scheduled for minor surgery. On top of these problems, I knew that by firing her she would lose all her benefits. It was an agonizing decision, and I begged God for a solution.

Throughout the year I had to continue routinely documenting the reasons for her inevitable dismissal, at the same time I was praying for her on a daily basis, that God would provide another way. There were a lot of emotions when I spoke to her about the legal process, and she wasn't happy about it. I hoped she would resign so we could at least be a reference for her to find other work, but since she insisted on remaining I had to follow through the legal procedure necessary for terminating a contract. It certainly didn't feel good, but I continued to sense it was something I needed to do as part of my responsibilities, and I was to push through without delaying. The night before the board meeting when I had to let her go I continued praying for the process. I was sitting at home feeling the weight of the decision, when I received notice that her dismissal had been put in place. My heart sank. It felt so painful to me. I continued praying. An hour later I suddenly got a revised report. In the new report the minutes had been changed from "dismissed" to "resigned." She had decided to call in and put in her resignation, before the job was officially terminated the next day. I sighed with relief, knowing this was a better option for her, and trusted that God would work through this tough situation. At the start of the next school year she was one of the first people to come to see me.

"You know, Mike, I just want to thank you. You doing what you did. I was so sick, and I just wasn't taking care of myself. Then when I lost the benefits I knew I was going to have to make lifestyle changes. Because of that, I didn't have to go through surgery. I got better naturally and am now feeling healthier than ever. So basically, you saved my life."

That same year we started an after-school program for kids, and I hired her husband to become the director of the program which he continued to do for many years. He also thanked me several times for what I did for his wife, helping her make a difficult transition which restored her health and boosted her quality of life. Even while following the Holy Spirit through a difficult and painful process, I believe that process of keeping her on my hotlist was what brought an incredible end-result to that story. I like to call it the PUSH method — when faced with a hard situation, I simply start "Praying Until Something Happens." Many times it seemed like I was in a dead end, with no good options left except to pray. Time and time again I would see God come through to surprise me with a unique solution of His own, much better than I could have foreseen from my own wisdom or perspective.

Practically, how can we step into situations of crisis that may look very overwhelming, and ugly? First of all, we need to deal with the expectations in our own heart. One of the things I was taught as an administrator, is that "when people come in angry and screaming and yelling at you, it's because they feel like they haven't been heard." In any line of work, we will face challenges, but I think a huge growth point for me happened when I began to make a conscious choice to recognize that many times when we are faced with difficult people or situations, it's because God has intentionally brought them to us. He is aware that they are in a point of crisis, possibly because He knows that deep down they are looking for hope, and change. Rather than just seeing it as something that we must endure to strengthen our own character, I think there's a special opportunity to ask God to use us to be His ministers of grace in that moment. What is the gospel message He wants to transmit through our life, to that person? Looking back over the years, I have come to value how rare and precious these moments can be, and they should not be easily wasted. Especially in the professional world, people usually have a guard up trying to appear that they have it all together. They will often mask what they are going through. When this wall comes down, what is behind it may not be very good to look at. Anger is often an emotion used to mask fear, insecurity, or pain. It may be an uncomfortable place to face, and yet it's a holy moment for them. It's important in these times to put our ego aside and resist the temptation to take their actions personally. As soon as I realize I am going into one of those moments, I pray and ask, "Holy Spirit, help me not be sidetracked by the drama. Help me recognize that this is a life-changing moment in their destinies." Everything could change in this one visit.

Randy Fisk spoke a sermon that really changed the way I did business. I remember he was teaching one Sunday about the beauty and awesomeness of God, and he said that our God is always doing something, always. We are limited by our own vision of things. We are so overwhelmed with stimuli that we have taught ourselves to not be distracted. There are so many shades of green, such clarity, such nuance, so many things going on around us. A lot of times people say that kids that are autistic are overwhelmed all the time by the stimulus, but God's voice is the same way, always speaking, always doing things around us, but we are just numb to it. We are so used to shutting it out. You don't have to wait for God to do something, He is ALREADY doing it, all around you.

A tip I learned from another administrator: I always carried an index card where I kept bullet points of the major things I had to get done that day. I always kept that in my pocket so if I was walking around the building I would say, "Maybe there's something I can knock out now." I could zip into an empty classroom so I could do it, pray over a specific classroom, pray Holy Spirit in this wing, for example.

I started thinking about my office at the job, so much stuff going on all the time, and all the battles I was seeing on a daily basis, when I realized these are actually spiritual battles. I realized I actually had power to affect a change, affect a difference, and it really increased my praying game. At this point, I started walking through the school every day in prayer, and creating the bookmark prayer cards. It is important to keep your mouth closed; don't feed into the drama, but stay connected to the Spirit. Try your best to listen to them and at the same time listen to the Holy Spirit. In the beginning when I first was a principal, I admit that I was mostly going through the motions, and trying to get through the "crisis" points of the day as quickly as possible in order to get back to my long to-do list for the day. I saw parents with problems as time-sucking burdens that were slowing me down from my real tasks.

The transformation moment in my life came when I realized that my work was more than just finishing my to-do list. The real call on my life, and my greatest impact as an administrator, was actually when I was able to affect change in people's lives. Of course, the last thing parents of a "bad" kid expect when they come to a school is to get personal prayer and ministry from the principal. They don't expect that in a million years. Rather than being yelled at or judged, they are listened to with compassion and care that extends beyond the needs of the school, to the needs that matter most to them. When parents have those kinds of encounters, everything changes. It almost always changes the student's behavior in the school, and I have seen a ripple effect across families and generations of students in our district. Some of our most disenfranchised families became pillars of support in our community that began helping other families. They become a resource to others, once I truly made myself a resource to them. As I started to follow the Holy Spirit, and saw the kinds of things He was capable of doing, my entire perspective of my job changed. I realized I didn't just need to minimize or push away the crisis, but Jesus could actually use me to be the answer to the problem. Once that soaked into my being, things really took off.

SUMMARY
Hard times are an opportunity for God to step in and show His power and love. In Jesus we see a man who is deeply compassionate, full of emotion, and acutely sensitive to the thoughts and feelings of people around Him. One of the things that sets Jesus apart is that He does not seem to be afflicted with anxiety and stress. He seems to be confident about God's timing, His provision, and His miraculous solution to any crisis.

REFLECTION
How do you react in crisis? What is effective and what is "an area for growth?" Are you willing to put into practice the PUSH method — when faced with a hard situation, you simply start "Praying Until Something Happens." Time and time again I would see God come through to surprise me with a unique solution of his own,

much better than I could have foreseen from my own wisdom or perspective.

ACTIVATION
- o Identify one challenge or crisis you are currently experiencing.
- o Pray for the situation or person every day for the next 21 days.
- o Place a sticky note or paper reminder to pray somewhere you will see it.
- o Ask God to show you one spiritual action you can take in that situation (meeting with someone involved, praying for them directly).

CHAPTER 5: OVERCOMING POWERS OF DARKNESS

Supreme excellence consists of breaking the enemy's resistance without fighting.
— Sun Tzu, The Art of War

When we think of the life of a great missionary or evangelist, we know they must have battled spiritual warfare to take new ground for Christ. By comparison, you might think life as an administrator in the suburbs of the Midwest would be pretty cut-and-dry. Over my years of working in Chicago school districts, I realized that the spiritual realm was something I could no longer deny.

My first wake-up call came in the form of a tiny six-year-old boy. He had been disrupting the classroom for weeks, acting out with rage and violence. When the buddy-system no longer worked, he ended up in my office and immediately hurled papers and decorations to the floor. Within minutes I was shocked to realize how quickly he had destroyed the place. I moved to restrain him but somehow struggled for at least twenty minutes to keep him from harm. When I finally had him in a chair, he began lifting office furniture off the ground, including the heavy desk he was sitting beside. I looked down in disbelief because it looked like it was being lifted by some six-foot-four bodybuilder. I shook my head suddenly and realized something beyond the natural was going on, there were probably demonic forces involved, and I should actually get some backup. For me, this was a dramatic awakening to the reality of demonic presence.

From that point on, every time I faced a similar situation, I would ask and pray, "Is this a demonic situation? Do I need to take authority over any unclean spirits and deal with them right now, or is this something that you are going to take care of?" If I got the sense that it was going to be dealt with later, then my normal thought process would be to ask, "What's the underlying cause of what's going on right now?" I believe that when we have this mindset, the Holy Spirit will often bring things to the surface and guide us to the root of the issue. In this way, I was able to effectively deal with many of the students and families that had struggled for years with behavior issues. We should never see these people as the problem; they are usually the ones that have suffered the most. When people are oppressed by demons, Jesus has deep compassion for them and wants them to be free. In one of the great passages about spiritual warfare, Paul urges us:

Michael D Smith

A final word: Be strong in the Lord and in His mighty power. Put on all of God's armor so that you will be able to stand firm against all strategies of the devil. For we are not fighting against flesh-and-blood enemies, but against evil rulers and authorities of the unseen world, against mighty powers in this dark world, and against evil spirits in the heavenly places.
Ephesians 6:10-12 (NLT)

Treating everything from simply a scientific or psychological approach actually gives away a lot of the real authority we have in the spiritual realm. Especially for people in a position of leadership or authority, I think it's important to act with both wisdom and knowledge of the authority we have in Christ. For me, it became clear over time that simply attacking it head-on was the most effective approach. It doesn't mean that every time people go into crisis there's a "demon." People have plenty of socio-emotional traumas that make life complicated and require gentleness and grace. I found the most helpful approach is actually a balance of both the natural and spiritual realms.

From my first encounters with miracles in Mexico, I was exposed to the supernatural role of healings and God, even though I didn't put my finger on it until later on. By the time I finished two Master's, I was really viewing everything from a sociological and methodical framework. As a principal, I had never really considered that some of these kids might be affected by demons. It wasn't something that was scary or overwhelming, but I realized it was probably foolish for me to try to handle this on my own. I called in a staff member and another Christian teacher and asked them to pray while I took a break. I don't believe that demons have the upper hand, but using a spiritual approach instead of struggling to control things from the flesh made a complete difference.

Taking a "spiritual" approach does not mean that we have to begin acting like weird gurus, carrying holy water or silver crosses around. It's actually quite simple. If you look at the weapons Paul describes, they are solid biblical principles that make for excellent leadership in any field: truth, righteousness, peace, faith, salvation in Christ, and the word of God. We are told to pray in the Spirit, to be prayerful, and to be alert.

> *Therefore put on the full armor of God, so that when the day of evil comes, you may be able to stand your ground, and after you have done everything, to stand. Stand firm then, with the belt of truth buckled around your waist, with the breastplate of righteousness in place, and with your feet fitted with the readiness that comes from the gospel of peace. In addition to all this, take up the shield of faith, with which you can extinguish all the flaming arrows of the evil one. Take the helmet of salvation and the sword of the Spirit, which is the word of God. And pray in the Spirit on all occasions with all kinds of prayers and requests. With this in mind, be alert and always keep on praying for all the Lord's people.*
> Ephesians 6:13-18 (NIV)

Similar to much of what I have described in this book when it comes to prophecy, healing, or evangelism, I simply rely on the Holy Spirit to guide my awareness and responses. Whenever I face a situation that doesn't look like Jesus, I ask, "Holy Spirit, what's going on? What do we need to deal with?" When I feel prompted to pray for deliverance, it's guided by the sense that the person wants to be free.

DELIVERANCE PRAYER
In this situation, with the six-year-old boy, we calmed him down, praying silently over any spiritual battle that was overtaking him. That day I made an appointment with his mother. I told her we had noticed unusual behavior in her son, and asked her if she had seen anything like that at home. She immediately confirmed that over the year he had become extremely erratic, spontaneously erupting with rage, foaming at the mouth, and moving on all fours. She didn't know what to do. I asked her if she had considered that possibly what was happening might be a spiritual attack of some sort, and told her that I thought the pastor of my church might be able to help him. She agreed that she would really like that. She also shared that her son's father was a gang member, and that her son had witnessed a lot of domestic violence in the home. She had seen him becoming a completely different person, and she had felt that it was a dark spirit attacking her son.

I asked her if she was Catholic, and she said yes, she attended Our Lady of Good Counsel. I told her to check with her priest, and get his okay. Over the years I often worked with the different pastors and priests in town, and we saw many families receive breakthrough and transformation. When she arrived on Sunday I introduced her to our pastor and the ministry team. At that point, I was concerned about creating a mixed world between my professional life and ministry, so I introduced her to our church's ministry team to pray with the family. After the service, they prayed with the son and his mother, and he was set free. From that point on, he became a normal, sweet student with no more problems in the classroom. And from that point on, God regularly began putting people in my path who were ready to be set free, healed, and saved.

Ironically, many Christians seem to think that in order to be used by God, they need to wait until God calls them into full-time ministry. As an administrator in the workplace, I felt there were way more opportunities to pray and minister when I was in my secular job than when I became a pastor a few years later. When working in a church or in full-time ministry, you often spend your time surrounded by Christians. Eventually, when I did become a pastor, I became aware that many people stopped opening up to me in the same way because they had preconceived ideas of who I was or how I might respond to them. When people knew I was a pastor, immediately walls went up. They didn't want prayer. Even people who were slightly religious might view me with suspicion, "No, I'm good. I got my own church. I got my own pastor." As a co-worker, or an ordinary professional, many people saw me as more relatable and were perfectly willing to share their problems with me or let me pray for them. Many times as a pastor you represent the embodiment of all the negative interactions anyone has ever had with a church. As a pastor offering prayer, some people think you might have to become a member of your church, give you tithes, or that you have a hidden agenda. In the marketplace, there was a lot more freedom. People seemed to receive the authenticity of the gesture for what it was.

Michael D Smith

As I grew in confidence and understanding that God was calling me to minister to the problems I encountered every day in my workplace, I naturally began to see deliverances happening on a regular basis. I also felt comfortable to pray with the students and families myself as issues arose, rather than wait to bring them to church. For some families, inviting them to church might create a barrier, or trigger fears of past negative experiences they have had with churches. They may already have a home church and feel a sense of conflicting loyalties. I always try to be sensitive to respect these relationships, as well as be aware of negative experiences people may have had. For other families, the church setting might offer them more of a sense of safety or protection than they feel in a school.

I had an interesting experience with a homeless woman who had two daughters who attended our school. This woman was battling a lot of addictions and was extremely volatile. One day she came into our office screaming and yelling and throwing a fit. I don't even know what it was about, but she had our entire office in turmoil. I called her into my office and asked her to sit down. She came in ranting and raving about everything going on in her life, spilling out all the problems she was dealing with. I prayed to the Holy Spirit to guide our conversation and bring freedom and peace to this woman. After listening for a while, I finally stopped her and asked, "What is the deeper issue here?" I think even she was starting to realize that she was rambling, and it wasn't making much sense. She told me that she was diagnosed as a paranoid schizophrenic and she hadn't taken her meds for a while.

I heard the Holy Spirit say, "Pray." When I asked permission, she agreed, and I felt led to pray against generational curses, and I cursed the illness of paranoid schizophrenia. As we prayed, a sense of peace fell over her and filled the room. My office staff was mystified to see her calmly and politely leaving the office that morning, all the stress gone and a lovely smile of peace on her face.

That weekend she showed up at our church and I thought, "Oh no! I hope she doesn't cause another scene here!" Actually, she stayed all the way through church and ministry time. Our pastor, Robby, went up to her and prayed with her. I went over to them just as she was telling Robby, "Well I know Mr. Smith. I met with him the other day in his office, and he started screaming and yelling at me telling me I had to come to church here."

Of course, I was horrified thinking, "I did no such thing!!!" Then I realized the Holy Spirit works in different people's situations and hearts, and He knew that for this type of woman to be able to respond, she was going to have to hear it in a loud screaming kind of way. Even though I had only briefly mentioned our church at the end of the prayer, the Holy Spirit made it scream out at her. That day she was delivered from meth addiction. She didn't want to talk in front of me, because she knew I was a mandated reporter. My pastor told her she was in a safe place in that church, so we both prayed with her.

PRECAUTIONS AND TIPS
When praying for deliverance, I try to pray with more than one person. It's helpful to have only one person speaking directly to

the person in need of freedom, while others simply pray. I never did this during school hours, but would set appointments after work. I never prayed with any child without their parent's permission. Whenever possible, I would also ask the parent to be there. Many times both the student and the parent were ministered to. As an educator and overseer, I don't meet with any staff member to pray with them during school hours. My office at the school has windows and the blinds are always open, doors unlocked. If I have a meeting or longer talk, I try to set that up in a public location like at a cafe. Choosing the right setting and place can be an important part of the preparation.

In Matthew 10:1(NLT), Jesus gives his disciples "authority to drive out impure spirits and to heal every disease and sickness." To pray for deliverance, I first invite the Holy Spirit, and bind any unclean spirit from manifesting. Basically, that means that I command the spirit to be silent in Jesus' name, and be still. This keeps things simpler, usually. Next, I command it to come out, get off the property and leave. Usually I can tell right away when the demon has left, because the person begins looking and acting differently. Sometimes their face color changes, their eyes change and can become brighter or lighter. Sometimes when the demons leave, the person may cough, sneeze, or spit up. I have seen some demons try to distract the person from praying, try to get them to leave or to fall asleep. These are more passive aggressive manifestations. You may not be completely sure as to whether the demon has left or not. To some level, you can only tell with time if someone has been truly set free. The next thing I do is pray with the person and, if they recognize what just happened, ask how do they feel. Help them to process and ask them if they would like to invite Jesus into that place in their life. Pray over the person and set up a follow through. Find out if they have a home church and if they are able to get follow through and help heal in the areas that might have been the entryway to demonic oppression in the first place. A helpful resource that offers a comprehensive biblical understanding as well as practical ministry applications is *The Biblical Guidebook to Deliverance* by Randy Clark, Ph.D.

HOW TO KNOW IF IT'S DEMONIC OPPRESSION
I think by the time you get to the point when you are noticing visible signs of demonic oppression, the person also notices it themselves. I think how you approach things is very important. There is no need to be dramatic or spooky about things. If you have a relationship with the person, and can call them aside privately, "I know you've been kind of 'off' lately, how are you doing? I believe God would like to bring more freedom and relief to your life, would you like to pray with me?" Whether a demon is "oppressing" someone, or "possessing" someone is beside the point. For me the purpose is to have that spirit leave, and to minister God's love, peace, and encouragement to that person. One of the good things about the workplace setting is that you will continue to see these people and ask how they are over time. In a workplace situation, the relationship is the ultimate goal. It's important to preserve the relationship, and approaching people with humility goes a long way to seeing this happen. Too many times I've seen Christians come in and burn bridges, arrogantly walking around and pointing out other people's errors and acting like they are above them.

With the deliverance, it's not much different than praying for healing, one is setting that person free from sickness, the other from a dark spirit. I don't see that much of a difference between the two. You do your part, and do what you've got to do. It might not just be a demonic thing, but there might also be severe mental health issues that require medication, counseling professionals, or social workers. If someone is in a place where they would be dangerous to themselves or others it's important to get help.

SUMMARY

I believe that when we have this mindset, the Holy Spirit will often bring things to the surface and guide us to the root of the issue. When people are oppressed by demons, Jesus has deep compassion for them and wants them to be free. It's actually quite simple. If you look at the weapons Paul describes, they are solid biblical principles that make for excellent leadership in any field: truth, righteousness, peace, faith, salvation in Christ, and the word of God. We are told to pray in the Spirit, to be prayerful, and to be alert. It might not just be a demonic thing, but there might also be severe mental health issues that require medication, counseling professionals, or social workers. The important thing is to stay dependent on the inner guiding voice of the Holy Spirit. He is able to guide us through the complexity of situations far beyond our understanding or rational solutions, whether dealing with the spiritual realm or politics in the workplace.

REFLECTION

What is your understanding of the battle against "the powers of this dark world and spiritual forces?" What stories or personal experiences come to mind? How has what I have shared affected your thoughts? Your concerns?

HOW TO PRAY AGAINST DEMONIC OPPRESSION
General guidelines that I have developed over the years:
- When meeting for prayer, set up a quiet place without interruptions, outside of working hours.
- I never pray with any child without their parent's permission. If possible, I try to have them get approval from their spiritual leader or pastor if they are members of another church or denomination.
- When praying for deliverance, I always pray with more than one person.
- It's helpful to have only one person speaking directly to the person in need of freedom, while others simply pray.
- Bind the spirit out loud and forbid it not to manifest or disturb in any way. I do this to help preserve the person's dignity. The enemy wants to make a fool of them.
- Command it to leave the person and the building. Pray for the Peace of Jesus to come, and invite the Holy Spirit to minister to that person.
- Sometimes the Holy Spirit may reveal where this demonic oppression started, and it might be an opportunity for them to forgive someone who hurt them, or receive inner healing.
- Check in with the person, ask them how they feel, and if they notice any difference. Sometimes there will be an obvious change, even in physical appearance, Other times it may be just feeling better or lightness.

- I always ask them if they would like to invite Jesus into their heart, even before the deliverance prayer if possible
- The important thing is to stay dependent on the inner guiding voice of the Holy Spirit. He is able to guide us through the complexity of situations far beyond our understanding or rational solutions.

CHAPTER 6: SPIRITUAL ATMOSPHERES AND THE POWER OF FORGIVENESS

"When you hold resentment toward another, you are bound to that person or condition by an emotional link that is stronger than steel. Forgiveness is the only way to dissolve that link and get free." – Catherine Ponder

Sometimes the most powerful breakthroughs happen when strongholds of unforgiveness and pain become released to Jesus. I was at a new school, and one of the individuals I worked with was a steely-faced woman who was in charge of the school before I came. She had a tough personality, and when she had an issue, she often dealt with it publicly, perhaps sending out mass emails cc'd to every staff member in the building, creating her own bulletin announcements, or even taking some issues straight to the press. We had gone to the same school and been part of the same teachers' union in Chicago, so she saw me as an ally in her "social-justice" campaigning. But there also tended to be turmoil in our interactions.

It was humbling to have small matters constantly amplified and broadcast before I had a chance to try to mediate any of the conflicts. "I don't know what she's dealing with or what she's going through," I told my wife, "but I've got to know her story, and find some things in common with her to build rapport." As I was able to find those connection points, she trusted me and started to come to me with some of her official complaints before publicizing them.

Over the years she became one of my staunchest allies, but every semester there were still layers of drama and intrigue. I continued to pray for her, my sister in Christ. One day after dismissal, while making my rounds of the classrooms, I came to her new reading center. We sat in the student chairs, chatting at first, but it turned deeply personal. She told me about how the night before a storm had knocked off some branches of a tree on the roof of their house. She was both worried and mad at her husband who was suffering from cancer, possibly terminal. Her husband had climbed up to take down the fallen branches, and she had lit into him, causing a huge scene in front of the neighbors. "I really flipped out on him," she admitted. "You know why I always have been so reactionary like that? Ever since I was a kid, an uncle that went to church with us used to molest me for years. I always felt so powerless, and after that I didn't want anybody to ever take any power over me again, you know what I'm saying? It's what made me who I am today, why I don't take no crap from nobody." When I asked her if she had ever confronted the family member, she told me, "Nah, he is dead already."

She looked down at the crucifix around her neck, fidgeting nervously and twirling it around again and again, running the cross up on its side. She was very tense. I realized that it was possible she had never told this to anyone before. It was a holy moment, and God was doing something. He had opened her heart. I always believe that God reveals to heal. When someone shares something so personal like that, it's because part of them wants to be free.

"You know, you don't have to live like this anymore." I looked at her. "You can give all these things to Jesus and He can set you free."

She nodded her head. "I'd like that."

"It's simple," I told her. "We can pray right now and God can release you from this weight."

"Holy Spirit, come. I break off the spirit of shame. Leave now. Anything that was stolen from your childhood I pray for restoration of those things. I pray for any dark cloud of oppression to leave, and depression and anxiety."

You could feel that the atmosphere of the room was different. It literally looked brighter. It had felt sort of dull and grey in that room, then it felt bright.

At that moment, it would have been hard to tell if anything had happened. But there was certainly a shift in her being, a calmness in her relationships with me and with the other staff. It's helpful to know that many times when I'm praying with people, a vast majority of times I do not feel or sense that anything is happening. By faith I believe something is happening. Occasionally there may be a reaction of tears, or a transformed face that looks lighter and full of joy, but many times I have no visual cues, I simply move forward in faith. I may not even personally feel anything when I am praying, but I trust that our words and prayers are being used by God for healing the heart. To me the best evidence is a transformed life, over time.

STANDING IN THE GAP
Another long-term teacher, Alan Voelkel, shared this story with me of a time when he felt called to stand in the gap of forgiveness for the hurt and pain he saw in his workplace. The following two stories are in his words.

Some years ago, our school principal moved on to another job and the staff assumed the responsibility of hiring a new leader. The school council devised an elaborate process to systematically identify the salient characteristics of the ideal administrator we wished to hire, and tasked the members with interviewing all stakeholders to ensure that every voice was heard.

As the family liaison my job was to interview the parents. After holding a spate of meetings to canvass the parents, it became obvious that a majority felt very strongly that the new principal should be, among other things, a male figure who could be a role model to the school's boys and a complement to the assistant principal who was female. We each presented the results of our inquiries at an all-day summit meeting some weeks later.

Inexplicably, after I shared my findings from the survey I felt a chill fall across the room. Suddenly one of my colleagues raised her voice and started growling at me. "I don't know why we would want a man to be the principal. It seems like men have done a pretty good job of messing up the world so far!" I was stunned as others at the table quickly picked up the chorus, denouncing men in general, and then focusing their ire and indignation at me.

"I'll bet you don't even wear the pants in your home," sneered another whom I barely knew. "You've got a lot of nerve coming here with your sexist views!" As vile, vindictive, and personal insults swirled around me, I found myself feeling defensive, wondering what I had done to deserve these personal attacks. Suddenly my mind flashed back to a sermon I had recently heard from a guy working in the field of racial reconciliation.

"It really doesn't matter if you or anyone else in your family ever had anything to do with

slavery and oppression," the speaker noted. "As Christians we have a unique opportunity to stand in the gap, as Christ did. Though He was without sin, He went to the cross and stood in the gap for us." The speaker paused. "Who else is going to apologize for those sins of racial oppression? The world?"

Looking at the angry faces of the women at that table, I knew that I had a singular opportunity.

"Excuse me ladies," I interjected with no small degree of trepidation. "I'd really like to say something."

Michael D Smith

The room grew quiet as I looked at each set of fierce, slitted eyes blazing back at me, daring me to speak. "I realize as I look around this room that there is a lot of hurt here caused by men," I said, almost in a whisper. "Some of you have had fathers and brothers and husbands and colleagues who have lied to you, taken advantage of you, cheated on you, abandoned you, perhaps even abused you. Some of you have been unfairly passed over for jobs by men who were less qualified than you, and yet you were discriminated against just on the basis of your sex. All of that was hurtful, wrong and unjust, and there was no excuse for it.

"Those men are not here today, but if I may humbly speak on their behalf, I want to tell you how sorry I am for what has happened to you.

"I want to sincerely apologize for the indignities that you have suffered for which there is no excuse, and I want to beg your forgiveness from the bottom of my heart. You deserved much better."

All the air was instantly sucked out of the room and the cosmos stood still. No one said a word. Glancing up at the eyes in the room, I remember that most had averted their gaze, some rimmed with tears. We sat there in silence for several minutes until the moderator quietly suggested that we take a break. A week or two later I received a note from one of the women who had been the most hostile. She didn't mention the event, but she did describe how she had once attended church as a child with a friend, and that something about me had given her a desire to get reconnected with her faith.
Did I know of a church that I could recommend for her?

Six months later I attended her baptism, and a decade later she is now a leader in her church. When I see her, I am reminded of the great privilege God gave me that day to stand in the gap and to speak words of healing and contrition to that group of hurting people.

Alan also shared with me that he realized that without releasing forgiveness from his own heart, he had created a spiritual barricade that was blocking his work and keeping him from being used by God. Here is his story:

There was one cardinal rule for all the club sponsors and coaches who worked in the district: "All funds raised by students MUST be deposited in the Student Finance account." No exceptions. Yearbook sales. Ad sales. Fundraisers. Donations. It didn't matter the source. It all had to be deposited in the bank on a timely basis in the Student Finance account.

The most intractable and maddening feature plaguing the system was trying to get the money back when you needed it. You had to fill out the right forms. You had to make your purchase from a list of officially sanctioned businesses. Or if there wasn't one, demonstrate that you researched competitive bids from at least three different vendors.

The next hurdle was to have the paperwork signed by the appropriate administrators, the sponsor and several student representatives whose signatures had to be on file downtown. Included in the packet must be documentation proving that the sponsor, after first holding an election of officers, held a series of official club meetings with the kids to discuss and approve the purchase following a meticulous, predetermined process. Once assembled and copied in triplicate, the sponsor mailed the entire packet to the central office where it could take weeks or even months to find out if the purchase was approved and even more time to then be processed and submitted to the vendor. Quite often it would suddenly all be returned for some trifle. Perhaps the student who was elected to be the club treasurer disappeared from school and the new kid who replaced him did not have his signature on file downtown. Start over again. It could be very frustrating. It was not uncommon to receive your order at the start of the following year after the original students who approved the purchase were long gone. While this might make sense for lucrative contracts and the purchase of heavy equipment, most club expenses were simply for small things like snacks for the kids, some T-shirts, miscellaneous supplies, a new ball or maybe a field trip. The system was so cumbersome and time intensive that most teachers simply resorted to spending their own money to avoid the hassle. It simply wasn't worth the headache and the runaround.

Most teachers I knew dipped into their personal funds to purchase classroom supplies, so the idea of even asking the school to buy my class computers was a hopeless pipe dream. Instead, I had worked all year aggressively fundraising through ad sales, student fundraisers and Arizona Tax Credit donations. One memorable day my requisition for a computer purchase came back to me in the familiar reusable manila envelope used by the district originating from the Student Finance office. Ripping it open with eager anticipation, my enthusiasm suddenly collapsed when I spotted a stamp at the top of the packet which hit me between the eyes like an electric shock. "Denied."

I rifled through the paperwork, desperately trying to spot what grievous error I must have committed. But everything was in order. Mystified, I ran back to my office to bang out an email to Barbara, the lady who handled our account at Student Finance. I tried mightily to disguise the rising sense of irritation and outrage burning inside me. Barbara was all business. She explained that it was "inappropriate to use Student Finance funds for computer purchases since it is the job of the district to provide computers to the schools." Come again?

The district had no money for classroom computers, let alone a journalism lab. How else were my students supposed to get the hard-earned computers they needed and had fundraised to earn all year long? She responded that she was well aware of all of that, but that she was simply following the policies of Student Finance. Sorry. It was a catch-22.

I blasted a machine gun load of frantic emails out to sympathetic administrators in a desperate attempt to enlist their support. They all expressed sympathy and regret, but assured me that there was nothing they could do. That was the system. I was beat. With no options left to pursue on this front, I started writing letters to see if I could get friends and family to donate their old computers as an alternative. Of course, it wouldn't be the same, but what else could I do? The forty thousand dollars we had fundraised all year for new computers was gone.

One Sunday morning several weeks later I was confronted by a sermon at church on the topic of forgiveness. The pastor went for the jugular: challenging us to picture the faces of people who we needed to forgive. If God can forgive us for all that we've done, should we not forgive others in the same measure?

Of course, the image of Barbara's face zoomed to center stage in my imagination. I was still furious with her and at night I tossed and turned. I could feel it eating me alive. Chastened, I resolved to do the right thing. I would try to forgive her.

Michael D Smith

Later that week I purchased a bouquet of a dozen roses and left them at the front desk with instructions that they be delivered (anonymously) to her office. Along with the bouquet was a typed note thanking her for all that she did to help the students at the schools receive the things that they needed. The note also acknowledged that hers was a thankless task, likely unheralded and insufficiently appreciated. I thanked her for her service and her sacrifices.

I admit that I bought the bouquet and wrote the note through clenched teeth. However, as the words flowed onto the page, a tiny crack appeared in my wall of rage and a few drops of sympathy spilled out.

A few days later while driving home, my thoughts returned to Barbara and the others in the Student Finance office. I wondered what it was like to work in their windowless world shuffling papers all day long from people and places that they knew only from the dry words on the forms and from a few terse e-mail exchanges. Buy this. Order that. All these disembodied requests unattached to any firsthand knowledge of the beating hearts and stirring stories behind them. They knew nothing of the kids and their challenges. They would never savor the thrill and excitement that the fruits of their efforts generated in the young people receiving the benefits. To see the wonder in the eyes of the kids and to bask in the joy of watching students burst into the classroom for the first time, marveling at the unimaginable surprises and new worlds that awaited them. Nothing like that, ever. For them it was all commodities, purchase orders, serial numbers, and balancing accounts. Did the order include the cost of taxes and shipping? All about the bucks with none of the bang. And if the transactions did generate any personal exchanges, quite likely they were mostly of the complaining, exasperated sort. "I need this yesterday!" "You screwed up!" *Perhaps even when they didn't. It was a job that someone had to do, but I couldn't imagine how it did not drive them insane.*

Suddenly, I felt a measure of compassion for them all. Their job was like chewing food but without the pleasures of taste and aroma. It was like hard work without the paycheck at the end. It was like sleeping without dreaming. It was a black and white existence. It was like reading a romance novel but with the last few chapters missing: the part of the story where all the subplots get drawn together, the conflicts resolved and the narrative tied up with the bow of a happy ending and a sunset. It was like living life but with all the moments of joy and happiness squeezed out, leaving just the desiccated, residual, mundane, boring bits.

I realized that I had it within my power to put some of the color, the flavor and the pay-off back into their tasks. I had the stories, but had I ever shared them with this team in the central office who helped to make it possible? Never once. That weekend I wrote a long letter to Barbara. It began with a paragraph describing how unfair it was that she never was able to enjoy "the end of the story" or to even know details of the context of the school site where the purchase orders she processed originated. I told her it was my intention in this letter to pull back the curtain and let her see it.

I described in detail my journalism class and the students in it. I told her about our publications, and what was unique about them. I pointed out the ways in which the things that she helped purchase for us were so key to our success and instrumental in achieving the quality both of the products we created and of the experience for our kids using them. The narrative included many stories so as to help Barbara imagine my students and their lives. I let her know how much I loved these kids and what they meant to me.

I told her the story of that Special Ed student with the artistic talent who became such a gifted cartoonist by using the drawing tablet with the computer and how it so profoundly impacted his relationship with his mother.

I described the newfound respect she had for him in light of her other son who was such a high achiever, and how it brought tears to my eyes to see him nourished by her respect. I included a copy of our latest Zine magazine with one of his cartoons for her to enjoy. At the end of the letter I thanked Barbara for all that she did to help us and hoped that she might feel proud for her role in helping to change kids' lives for the better. I signed my name and mailed it off to the Student Finance office.

A week went by and there was no response. Nothing. I waited another week and then began to get nervous. What was going on? I sent her an email with an unrelated question, but got no answer. I checked to make sure she still worked there. Had she even received my packet? My mind began spinning scenarios.

Weary of the wait, one afternoon I swung by the central office on the way home and nervously walked up to the Student Finance office on the second floor.

The place was torn up: all the pictures off the wall, furniture missing, piles of boxes stacked in heaps and trash cans overflowing. Grumbling custodians wielding dollies, under the watchful scrutiny of fastidious secretaries, moved in teams towards the service elevators. I caught one of the ladies to ask if Barbara was there. She pointed me towards her office. I found Barbara and another lady inside loading binders into boxes. "Oh, hi!" she said wearily. "We're moving. We're getting relocated downstairs." I asked if she could spare a moment to chat and she said that she could. Was there a private space we could use? She had me follow her to a nearby vacant office where we closed the door and sat on some stacked boxes. "What's up?" she asked me.

I thought for a moment, fumbling for words and wondering where to begin. Finally I just asked her, "Barbara, have I done something to offend you?" She looked at me quizzically and smiled faintly. "No. In fact, just the opposite." She was silent for a moment. "I loved the letter you sent me," she said at last. "I'm sorry that I haven't responded. It wasn't just because of the move. It was because it really hit me hard. You see, I have a brother who is intellectually disabled."

Then she told me the story of her brother and the challenges that his disabilities presented to her and her family. She described how much she loved him and how much he meant to her, and how much it pained her to see him struggle through life enduring the indignities and the disrespect of others. As she spoke, I could feel her pain and see the tears gathering in her eyes. I labored to swallow the lump forming in my throat. Finally she came around to my letter. "When I read the part about the special ed student in your class, all I could think of was my brother and how much I wished that someone along the way had reached out to him the same way you did with your student."
She smiled at me again. "Like I said, I loved your letter."

Then she asked why I would possibly think that I had offended her. I told her about my frustration in having my requisitions denied and not *understanding why that happened. She apologized and told me to resubmit. "Of course, we'll get you your computers," she said with absolute authority. Finally, I said goodbye. She gave me a big hug and thanked me again for the letter. Everything changed after that moment.*

In the years that followed, Barbara became my greatest advocate in the Student Finance office. Her emails always included a friendly hello and an inquiry about the kids. I noticed that suddenly my paperwork started to come back on a greatly reduced timeline. Sometimes she would write to let me know that she had found a better deal with a different vendor for the equipment I had recently requested. Whenever I had to drop things off at the office, her broad smile let me know that she was glad to see me and glad to help. I made sure to send her a personal copy of all of our school publications and to thank her for her support.

One fall, on a visit to the central office, I stopped by Student Finance just to say hello. I noticed that her office was vacant. "Barbara went back to the Midwest to be with her family," noted one of her colleagues when I asked for her. "We're really going to miss her here." I agreed. "Yeah, I'm going to miss her too!" I realized that I had just lost a member of my family.

I appreciate Alan's story, and it resonates with my own experience. Time and time again, I have seen simple gestures of kindness, gratitude, or service melt through hostile walls in just a few minutes, and destroy the strongholds of bitterness and hurt that the enemy has spent years building. My pastor Robby always says, "Love is a weapon of mass destruction." I believe as Christians we can often overlook that love, gratitude, compassion, and forgiveness are actually powerful supernatural tools to destroy the powers of Satan, just as prophecy or praying for the sick. As we follow the Holy Spirit's guiding, even seemingly simple acts of forgiveness, or gestures of kindness can transform spiritual atmospheres and bring powerful breakthrough.

SHIFTING SPIRITUAL ATMOSPHERES

As a school principal, I made it a rule to always arrive early and pray throughout the building at the start of the day. I believe that most of the time, our spiritual victories are won in our times of prayer. It doesn't mean that you have to be in your room praying on your knees, but simply walking throughout a building praying for the peace and presence of God to overcome every area of the building. The first school I was principal of was a foreboding 100-year-old brick building. I remember that when I first arrived some areas felt very dark and menacing to me. There were certain parts of the building I just wanted to run away from; they felt like places of fear. Each day as I unlocked the doors, I would pray for the Holy Spirit to fill the building and protect each person there. I would walk through the entire building each hour, and when I sensed any darkness I would pray in the name of Jesus for that to leave. Actually, one of the dark areas of the building, was also the classroom of one of the most difficult working relationships I had. When I first started as principal I was regularly being opposed and ridiculed by this person. I remember ever since I came into the school I had always prayed over that wing. As I regularly prayed over that area, I noticed also the teacher's relationship completely changed towards me. It felt like the barriers were removed and she began to come to me for help. In fact, over the next few years she became one of my biggest advocates. As Christians in the workplace I believe our role is to bring the reign of Christ wherever we go, releasing blessing, peace, and righteousness in our areas of influence.

One of the areas I often noticed seems to gather a heavier spiritual atmosphere is the teachers' lounge. Designed to be places of connection and rest, at many of the schools I worked at, I noticed they became dens of negativity and gossip. As a teacher I always avoided the lounge, and as a principal I did my best to target these areas to shift the spiritual atmosphere. I would spend a lot of time praying in those lounges and releasing peace. I physically spent time and energy to make it an attractive place, buying decorations, microwaves, and putting in vending machines with things teachers liked. I made a regular appearance there during my prayer walk and tried to be as hands-on as possible, taking care of the mail, sorting things that needed to be sorted, cleaning out the trash and washing the dishes, because it helped me be involved. It helped me be a contributor, not just a manager walking around. I believe there are spirits that can attach themselves to buildings, but through prayer and acts of love, we drive them out. I remember we had a school board president who liked to come to my building to visit me because she said that "my building was the only one like this that you could feel at peace." She said no other building was like that. That was my prayer, every time I would unlock the building I would pray, "Holy Spirit come and fill this school with Your presence." Before every staff meeting, I would pray as well. Some people live their lives in turmoil and stress, but we have authority to invite His presence and create an atmosphere of rest and peace wherever we go.

DEALING WITH WITCHCRAFT AND THE OCCULT

LEAP

I don't like to make too big of a deal about this, because it can be a distraction to see people as our "enemy" rather than as someone in need of God's love. Depending on the community you work with, witchcraft may be more blatant, or hidden. Many people would be surprised how blatant and common witchcraft has become. It's not just from foreign or rural cultures, but can be found in affluent American communities or mixed in with yoga and New Age practices.

One of my colleagues was a retired doctor who had worked at one of the top labs in the country. Both he and his wife were extremely well educated, he didn't need the money, he didn't want to be a teacher, but he liked me and working with the kids so he became my teacher assistant. He heard that I prayed for healing, and he asked me if I would pray with him. He told me how he had strange problems with his body that didn't have medical explanations and he had never been able to resolve. I remember praying with him. I felt like something had happened in his childhood that involved occult practices. He immediately told me when he was a child and his mother had taken him to a priestess instead of a doctor. She had rubbed an egg over his body, and opened it up and took out a chicken. He had always thought about that memory and associated it with his sickness, because since that time he had chronic pain and continuous health problems for over forty years. I prayed with him for the Holy Spirit to come. He had been a nominal Catholic, accepted Jesus that day and decided to check out a nearby Spanish church. In the next few weeks he told me the pain was gone, and he had a lot more energy. He's still alive and doing well today.

Michael D Smith

During my career in Chicagoland, there were a few points when I had direct encounters with witches in my workplace who specifically used curses against me and spells to try to drive me out of the area. It was at a new school I was working at where there had been a lot of turnover in the leadership. Looking back, I think I understand now some of the power dynamics, and some of the long-term staff members that preferred running the school themselves rather than having another boss to answer to. At the time, this was all new to me and I couldn't understand why I was having such a hard time, though I did notice a few unusual things that kept occurring. Several times I went into my office very early in the morning, and I could see that someone had been there before me. There was a strong smell of incense and sage only in my office, even though the school had been locked up over the weekend. During that time, I began experiencing headaches and migraines so severe that I was unable to go to work. It was the first time in my life that anything like that had happened to me. I found out later that this was a common practice used by a couple of known *brujas* in the neighborhood. People would pay them to put hexes and curses on people, and they would give them a special mixture to burn around the areas where that person was. What I knew was that I was battling fatigue and discouragement all the time, and I asked the prayer team at church to pray for me. Several people on the ministry team got pictures of spiritual warfare happening at my work and the need to break off curses and hexes. That same week my pastor left a voice message telling me that when he drove by the school where I work, he felt like the Holy Spirit showed him that there was witchcraft taking place there, and I should pray and break off word curses. I didn't want to jump to conclusions, but I had noticed that two of the women I worked with were really into shamanism, and seemed to have something against me. That same week, another intercessory friend sent me a prayer reversing any curses to go back to the person who sent them. This was the third confirmation from different people about the same thing, and I believe God was getting my attention as to what was going on. It was something I had never really considered before, but I was willing to try praying and see what happened. That weekend I prayed to take authority in the Spirit, praying that any curses set against me would be broken off and reversed to the people who had sent them. I felt better, like something finally lifted off of me. The migraines did stop soon after that, and I simply continued releasing peace over the school and praying for people who came across my path.

My leadership at this school was quite different than that of the past. I came in not needing a translator, but communicating directly to the parents myself. My hands-on approach connecting to community members somewhat displaced "how things had always been done." It was both a political and spiritual battle. I continued to pray for the school and practice servant leadership, intentionally taking on a lot of the grunt work like delivering mail, carrying packages. I spent a lot of time walking around the school and checking-in on staff and parents. Over time the staff saw the care I showed with the families, praying with a lot of the parents and the teachers with very positive results. I believe our best acts of spiritual warfare are simple acts of love, staying low and humble in the flesh, as we pray powerfully with faith in the spiritual realm.

Michael D Smith

One of the things I have always enjoyed doing since I was very young, was getting something old and broken and fixing it again. Whether it was a bicycle, motorcycle, snowmobile, or car, I loved getting the old parts working again, and seeing it run like new. In my younger years this had been how I made money. As an administrator, I had the same passion. As a teacher, I started taking the out of control classrooms and getting them in shape, then moving to another classroom. Working in difficult neighborhoods with scarce resources, I enjoyed putting together systems and teams to get the schools running smoothly and helping revive the community. I believe the enemy thrives in chaos, disorder, and trauma. As we start to bring order and peace to situations, we will often come up against spiritual strongholds that want to retain their control. People are not our enemy. Sometimes the ones that resist us the most are the very reason God sent us there to encounter His love. Over the years I have seen witches, gangsters, anti-Christian activists, and New Age gurus give their lives to Christ. Many of them have been deeply rejected and hurt by the church. A wise friend once told me that the best deliverance method is simply love. When we love the lost, when we show humility and respect and kindness to the people that mistreat us the worst, we are doing massive destruction to the kingdom of darkness. It may look like a simple act of compassion, patience, or acceptance, but what the enemy sees is carnage and destruction to his strongholds. As we live by the Spirit, we are helping bring freedom, restoration, and reconciliation to God's lost sons and daughters.

I believe in whatever line of work you do and whatever ministry situation you find yourself in, the important thing is to stay dependent on the inner guiding voice of the Holy Spirit. He is able to guide us through the complexity of situations far beyond our understanding or rational solutions, whether dealing with the spiritual realm or politics in the workplace. A powerful promise in Scripture I have always depended on is Isaiah 30:21 (NIV). *"Whether you turn to the right or to the left, your ears will hear a voice behind you, saying, "This is the way; walk in it.""* If you want to be used by God, my advice is to see your job, your neighborhood, or wherever God has placed you, as your full-time ministry, and simply begin to pray in situations you find yourself in, asking the Holy Spirit what is going on, and what He wants you to do.

The important thing is to stay dependent on the inner guiding voice of the Holy Spirit. He is able to guide us through the complexity of situations far beyond our understanding or rational solutions, whether dealing with the spiritual realm or politics in the workplace.

SUMMARY
In scripture we are told that our battle is not against flesh and blood, but against powers, principalities, and spiritual forces of darkness. Many times we may be tempted to view difficult people, relationships or situations from a worldly point of view, and even fight back in the flesh, trying to defend ourselves or even attack the other person or situation. In this chapter there were several examples to encourage us to see the spiritual battle that might be taking place behind the scenes, and it describes the way in which simple acts of love, forgiveness, or kindness might shatter a powerful spiritual stronghold.

REFLECTION

As you read through this chapter, how did it change your view of what spiritual warfare, or spiritual strongholds might look like in your life? Is there a time that you were impacted by a simple act of kindness, or an apology?

ACTIVATION

Take a few minutes and ask the Holy Spirit to bring to mind any situations where you have seen the fruits of unforgiveness, bitterness, tension, gossip or general darkness present. Next to each situation, write down what your response has been. Next, take a few minutes to pray and ask the Holy Spirit if there is a way He would like you to respond that could bring a breakthrough of love, forgiveness, compassion or encouragement to that situation. This week, make a commitment to use these spiritual tools to shift an atmosphere of darkness in your daily life.

CHAPTER 7: BACKDOORS OF HEAVEN

The essence of strategy is choosing what not to do. — Michael Porter

Kairos is an ancient Greek word meaning the right, critical, or opportune moment. A few years after I had surrendered my career to be used by God in any way He wanted, I noticed that He began to extend my realm of influence not just from the classroom to the campus, but at opportune moments across our district and into the political realm. I believe when Jesus prays, "Let Your will be done on earth as it is in heaven," He literally is commissioning us to be a transforming grace to society. If you look at American history, every major reform was led and brought about by Christians. From ending child labor, establishing the first public education, ending slavery, giving women the right to vote, and the civil rights movement – each of these important movements was led by evangelical Christians, carrying a calling and vision from God, and a compassion to see justice and truth established in this world. God is searching for people whose hearts are fully His. When we don't put limits on God, He doesn't put limits on the ways He can use us.

SPIRIT OF WISDOM IN A WORLD OF CHAOS

During my time as principal there was a massive uproar in our district. One of the district employees had snuck in a clause legislating highly controversial transgender rights policies. She had worked with Illinois Safe Schools Alliance, an LGBT youth advocacy group, to develop the policy. They gave her a proposal which they had drafted with the help of a national organization trying to establish new gender-neutralizing norms nationwide. In this case, however, rather than introducing it as a new policy, it was folded into a clause being presented as a "routine" policy update being approved by the board in order to comply with statewide anti-bullying requirements. The board of course had approved it, but without having any idea that it was mandating radical changes across the district, without any preparation or warning. Locker rooms were suddenly available to any student according to their gender preference, all staff were mandated to address every student according to their chosen pronoun preference, and a privacy clause would keep parents from being notified of their child's gender choice.

Needless to say, this did not go over well in a largely conservative suburban neighborhood bordering Naperville, Oswego, Geneva, Illinois. The board first found out about the new policy when the national media flew in to congratulate and interview them on the radically inclusive gender-fluid stance they had made, one of the first in the nation. East Aurora is largely traditional Hispanic

Catholics, and suddenly we had angry parents swarming the head office, worried that boys would be allowed into their daughters' showers and changing rooms.

Meanwhile protests had broken out in the community, angry parents were already pulling their kids out of school, while at the same time CNN, gay activists, and ACLU lawyers from around the country had flown in to try to make this a national case. This was in the fall of 2012, four to five years before any of these issues started to become part of the political battlefield in education. Literally thousands of emails and calls were flooding in, while petitions went up for and against the decision. I personally knew the leaders who were in the bullseye of the controversy, and how painful it was for them to be in a situation that they had technically approved.

The staff member responsible for writing the policy and getting it passed was placed on administrative leave, and didn't take any interviews. All of the fire was on the
superintendent and board members who were suddenly forced to face the wrath of people from every side of the issue, outside of the community, and in the national spotlight. They argued back that their district had never had complaints against LGBT bullying, and that the policies in question were unfeasible and unenforceable at the beginning of a school year, without any preparation or training in place. It was a difficult position to be in and, in response, the board began a tour of each of the schools in the district, to meet with the local communities directly affected. We set up a staff informational meeting at our school.

Outside the air was cool and the explosion of fall colors welcomed the new school year. Inside, instead of the fresh optimism that usually cheers the start of any school year, the room was filled with anger and disillusionment. I looked across the sea of faces and could feel how much it meant to everyone in the room. It felt like a personal battle for every individual that seemed to recall a haunting pain. Families on both sides of the issue had lost teenage relatives to bullying and suicide, and felt that this policy would create even more vulnerability. Some of the women who I knew had suffered assault and abuse were stricken with fear that the bathrooms and locker rooms would suddenly become places for predators. Others carried disappointment from having been marginalized in bigger city school districts, only to move out to our suburb and feel that their voice was invisible when these decisions were made without any discussion.

As my eyes scanned the crowd of familiar faces, I caught sight of the elected official who suddenly had to be the answer to all that pain in the room. I could see how deeply she cared, and I sensed her connection and love for this community. Usually when people like her end up in our kind of school district, it's because they want to deeply serve the needs of families who are really struggling. I could see this weighing across her face and body throughout the meeting.

After the meeting I made a point to reach out to her and offer some sympathy. I wished so much I could help take some of the pressure off her. I think she sensed this, and she was honest when I asked her how she was, "Things are going horribly for me." A few times in the past when times were difficult I had offered to pray but she had been very distant. This time she looked suddenly relieved and said, "Yes, that would be great." We sat in my office, out of the way of the crowds. Her face looked strained and sleepless. We actually talked about her prayer life, and I asked her what her relationship with God was like. She had grown up in the church until her mother died, and then she pretty much walked away from it. I could feel God's compassion for what she had been through, feeling like she was alone. I knew God wanted to meet her, and protect her through this time of battle.

I wasn't sure how she would respond, but I did feel a sweetness of the Holy Spirit present, and so I went ahead and asked her "Would you want to pray right now to encounter God again?"

She smiled and nodded slowly, "Yes, I would."

Outside the murmur of voices, shrieks, and impatient cars continued to battle in the parking lot. Behind me, an old radiator hummed and clanked, today's to-do list sat undone in a stack, and a pile of unsorted parent notices lay waiting for delivery. Although the day had been a hectic timeline, with people pressing all around, for that moment in the office, it felt like time stopped. A strong sense of peace settled. As we prayed, a thick presence of God filled my office. The atmosphere felt electric, yet full of His love. I know it wasn't just me, because I saw a clear stream of tears sliding down her face. She looked younger, suddenly lighter. "Do you feel that peace?" I asked her slowly. "How would you like to feel that all time?"

She said she would love that. I explained to her the salvation message, and she welcomed Christ into her life. We finished praying and continued talking. I suggested a couple of churches in her area where I sensed she would find community, and emphasized how the same presence she felt right now, she had access to all the time. I encouraged her to grow that connection by spending time with God each morning in prayer, and taking a few minutes to listen to His voice. I knew it was a rare moment, but one that I believe God had especially prepared for her.

Thirty minutes later I got a call. I had not been expecting to hear from her again, but she gave me her personal email address and she asked me to send a transcript of our prayer. Coming from a Catholic background, she felt most comfortable with following a sort of liturgy for prayer.

That same week, the woman who had written the policy and gotten it approved, called me and asked if she could come in to meet with me. She came in the back entrance and asked that I not let anyone know that she was there. "If only we had placed her in your school, she huffed, I am sure you would have embraced her needs as a trans-curious youth, and made him feel loved and welcomed just as he is. None of these problems would ever have to happen." She was referring to the student that had been the source of concern regarding the bathrooms and other gender-identity policies.
She sighed in front of me, her face tense and her shoulders sagging.

"I know how much you care about the kids," I reassured her, "and how much all of this has weighed on you. Are you okay?" As she began sharing her frustration and point of view, the outer exterior that had always been so angry and hard, softened. Underneath her tough exterior, I saw how much compassion she carried for kids who struggled to fit in, and were trying to understand who they were. She wanted to be their defender, and make sure that they were valued and accepted regardless of what they were going through. The divides in our district ran very deep, and loyalty came at a price, yet through the ministry of the Holy Spirit, God had brought an impact into the very heart of this divide. That day I saw God work through the situation powerfully and minister healing and restoration. As quickly as the issue came up, it was dealt with quickly and then seemed to have disappeared by the following month. I believe that in every battle we face, the true victories are won through prayer and being able to continually stay in awareness of God's love for the people around us, whether or not we agree with them.

In all of the infighting and political battles happening behind the scenes, sides were chosen with polar opposite beliefs and agendas. Ironically, in each of the crises that our district faced, each side reached out to me for prayer and support. They were both so hurt and angry at the other side, and what amazed me is that even though I had my own very strong convictions on the issue, God filled my heart with grace for each person that sat in front of my desk, and guided my prayers to encourage and restore them. Many times it was the very people that had persecuted and criticized me. By praying for them faithfully on a daily basis, and never speaking badly or criticizing them, God transformed the relationship into a place of ministry. I believe had I not stayed on my knees in prayer, or held my tongue when I wanted to criticize or voice a complaint, I would not have had the access and trust that I did when that *kairos* timing of God presented itself.

Although I was never someone that made the news, or held an elected position, I am surprised to look back and see how God used me with key administrators and leaders, at each of the pivotal moments our district went through. I believe that when God calls us to be salt and light in the world, He will often use this influence to release grace at specific times that only He knows about. I believe that when we cultivate a lifestyle of prayer and spiritual awareness, combined with ACTION, we make ourselves ready for these moments when they arrive.

Some of my favorite heroes of Biblical history are those we often see living quiet lives of faithfulness and obedience, until their *kairos* moment comes. As a principal, I have always believed in this principle of showing up every day and giving your 'A' game, doing the best work possible. Resisting difficulties and overcoming obstacles builds resilience. Sometimes there is the temptation to give in to apathy or complacency thinking, "It doesn't really matter anyways." When I think of men and women of excellence, who lived with integrity, I see the many times they were the ones that were chosen out of their generation for a special purpose. Some of the many examples of this in the Bible are Jacob, Joseph, Daniel, David, Ruth, Rebecca, Sarah, Abraham, Esther, Mordecai, and Mary. Each of these people worked hard and had found favor in society, but each of them reached a moment when God had them step out in faith and lay it all on the line. Their character and their work ethic complemented God's favor on their life, but it was their willingness to sacrifice their own position and comfort when the miraculous broke in. If you notice in the gospels, Jesus told his disciples, "Follow me," but never gave them any clue what would happen next.

> *As Jesus was walking beside the Sea of Galilee, He saw two brothers, Simon called Peter and his brother Andrew. They were casting a net into the sea, for they were fishermen. "Come, follow Me," Jesus said, "and I will make you fishers of men." And at once they left their nets and followed Him.*
> Matthew 4:18 (NLT)

Many times we can become so entangled in the "nets" of daily life in the workplace – the competition, stress, petty quarrels, ambitions, and even honorable duties – that we forget our true calling is to fish for men. Rather than getting caught up in the small perks and success that the world craves, we must be attentive and sensitive to what God's perspective is. During another tense time in our district, there was a leader who was being heavily criticized for actions and some unfortunate press. This person was not very popular, and the events of the year had only exacerbated the situation. I am sure she must have felt very alone at that moment. We were in a meeting together one time discussing these problems, and when the moment was right, I asked if she wanted to pray. I received a quick "No," and I dropped it. I didn't want to be pushy. After a few days passed and I kept getting the insistent feeling like I had a word of knowledge for this woman. "Okay Lord, if you want me to speak to her again, please make it plain and obvious to me and make it natural so I don't have to force it."

In my graduate studies, I learned of Dr. Ruby Payne, a sociologist. She talked about the disconnect of socio-economic problems in our country. According to her, many issues that from the outside seem to be race problems are actually socio-economic struggles. Most people who work in education are middle class, with a college degree but, especially in Title I schools, the communities they serve struggle with extreme poverty and almost no education. The challenge comes from bringing middle class expectations and forcing them onto people in poverty who don't have this same background. She offers solutions as to how to overcome this issue, and she talks about what we are doing wrong as middle-class educators. If someone would embrace this understanding in our school district, it would change everything. As the Holy Spirit had started leading me to take a much more active role with the families who attended our school, He was giving me a new perspective. I felt like He was reminding me about the course I took, and the key phrase "A framework of understanding poverty" to share with this elected official. Sometimes when I pray for someone, I use the "PUSH" method, Pray Until Something Happens. I write down the name, and I put it in a place like my Bible. I follow a Bible in a Year plan, and I put the paper right with my plan, and then say a quick prayer for that person or situation.

A few weeks later I was invited to a business breakfast in Aurora, and there were hundreds of people there, community leaders and business people. The place was huge, a lot of chatter and paper coffee cups in every direction. I grabbed a quick plate of food and scanned for a place to sit. I didn't know anybody. The woman who I was praying for saw me and she jumped up and started waving her arms and calling me to sit next to her. I knew the Holy Spirit had set up this meeting. Just then the school board president and another board member waved me over to the empty chair next to them, where the official was also sitting. Somehow in that moment the exact topic of conversation came up, and I was able to deliver my whole message to her, and the strategy that God had put on my heart during these several weeks in prayer. Though my message was for her, the other two men responded enthusiastically and requested copies of Ruby Paine's book. The woman wasn't a very popular or well-liked official, so it was hard for her to always be on the spot and taking the heat in the press. Delivering this message in front of the other men and having it so well-received by them created a beautiful open door. In fact, this word of wisdom at the right time gave me a lot of favor in her eyes. It impacted our relationship over the long term because she felt encouraged and supported. In conversations we had later, I could see that it had given her a lot of hope in a difficult moment. My belief is that even though she wasn't very popular in the moment, God's hand was over her leadership to shake things up in a good way.

I believe as we are willing to pray into the prompting of the Holy Spirit, He will provide the way. Sometimes in prayer I've found it helpful to write down some possible things to say, and rehearse a few of them so they would be fluid in my mind. When the time comes up, I pull out that card (mentally). For me, I usually look for an opportunity simply to pray with the person. I always invite the Holy Spirit to be present, and I've found that He often provides just the right words for that situation. The Holy Spirit is the best evangelist, and I find that in the presence of God, many times the fears or masks or different things that block people from connection, seem to simply fall away. My job is to invite people to simply open that door. Once people experience that presence of God, it's far better than anything I could do to try to persuade or convince anyone theologically. Although I usually try to recommend a way to connect again to a church, or another Christian co-worker I know could help them, many times I have seen that the Holy Spirit actually does a better job of following up than I ever could.

GREATER RISK, GREATER GAIN

I remember one of the first big steps of risk that I made was responding to a prompting I got that I needed to pray with the district superintendent. It was right in the beginning of this journey, when I had first resolved to stop just believing God could use me to do miracles, and start living in a way that expected them to happen. I was sitting at my desk in the summer typing on my computer when I got the persistent feeling to call him, though I didn't know why. I picked up the phone and set up a meeting for 1:00 p.m. I had been hoping to be able to plan what I wanted to say, but I really had no clue. As I drove there, I started praying for the Lord to guide me in this meeting. When I arrived at his office, he was in a lot of pain and having a problem with his eyesight; it's a genetic disorder in his family and it had deteriorated so much that the doctor had planned an intervention. Rather than have to fabricate something, God allowed me to simply respond to what was going on in his life in that moment.

I asked him if we could pray for healing and he agreed. He said he would be happy to be healed. I had him focus on a picture at the back wall of the office with his eyesight, and began praying for healing and breaking off generational curses.

As we started to pray he said he could feel electricity in the room when we were praying so he knew something was happening, but he didn't know what it was. We prayed together for about forty minutes with no change to his eyesight, and then I left. Later when he went to see his doctor for an exam, the doctor told him that strangely, rather than continuing to regress and worsen as it had been doing, his eye had dramatically improved. I told him how I had recently experienced a change in my theology that allowed me to experience a lot more of God working in my everyday life. This experience changed our relationship, and after that he asked me to please keep him on his prayer list. We began to meet regularly and pray once a month for guidance in the many decisions he was facing districtwide. This continued throughout my time as principal, and one day his secretary asked me about it. She said, "What are you guys doing there?" I always try to practice discretion, so I just mentioned that I liked to meet with him from time to time. "That's interesting," she mused. "You're the only person that he meets with. All the people in the central office were curious and wanted to know what you guys meet about."

"Oh, not much," I answered. From my point of view, I was doing heaven's business, and that only God knew what He was accomplishing through these times of prayer together.
Paul tells us we are to be soldiers, and soldiers would never become involved in civilian affairs. I believe that when we set

ourselves apart for God's purposes in our workplace, he will use us in extraordinary ways.

Another night, I had a vivid dream of a director of a department. This was someone I didn't know very well but who I could tell was very far away from sharing the faith that I had. It's not that he would ridicule me, but his comments would make clear that he had found a more enlightened way. The dream was very intense, and seemed to be a warning. In the dream I saw that he had a C clamp on his head on his temples and it was being screwed really tightly. I woke up from the dream gasping at the reality of the scene, and how vivid it was. I believed there was a message in it, but I thought to myself, "This is the last guy who is going to be able to receive this from me! I know he's not a Christ-follower, He's definitely going to think I'm crazy." I had to stop myself from embracing a cynical view of him. I have learned over the years that God sees a very different picture than we do. Some of the people I think are going to be the last ones to become Christians, are actually the most soft-hearted people who become huge evangelists themselves. As I brushed my teeth that morning, I resolved myself that if he seemed far from God, then actually that was probably the reason why. But I realized no, that's why I needed to pray for him. Before that, I don't think he ever reached out to me, in fact we had never spoken personally. I was at a point in my faith where I trusted that if God had chosen to reveal him to me in a dream, it's because he knew the man's heart and wanted me to reach out to him in some way.

LEAP

After praying about it, I simply called him and I told him, "I had a dream about you. I'm not sure what it means but are you having headaches or anything I could pray for?"

"No, why do you ask?"

I told him about the dream. "Would you like to pray?"

"No."

"Alright."

I hung up and that was that. It was a little awkward for me, but I felt committed to respond when I felt the Holy Spirit speaking.

A few weeks later a crisis hit, and he came to me to pray for him and for his wife who had been in a car accident. I am glad that I reached out to him when I did. When the crisis came, he knew who to call. After that time of prayer, I added him to my list of people I prayed for daily. It was not something I spoke about to other people. My philosophy was simply to do the stuff. I didn't often talk about what I did, but I privately committed myself each morning to be used by God in any way that he wanted. Sometimes people ask me if I was persecuted because of my faith, or made fun of. I didn't have a whole lot of ridicule from people because if they weren't involved in it, they didn't know about it. There were just a couple of people who believed they had been self-awakened and didn't have room for God in their lives. I was always an efficient administrator and competent employee, so I knew that if

I ever got a snide comment, it was usually more of a spiritual issue.

When the crisis hit our school district that I spoke about in the last chapter, and suddenly the pressure was on and CNN was in front of the Central office, surrounded by furious parents and chanting protestors, I received a call from this man. I was surprised when my secretary told me who was on the phone. "Hi, how can I help you?"

The voice on the other end of the line asked me if I had some time that morning, would I be willing to come down to the central office and pray with him. "When you come, use the back door," was his only request.

I know everybody on the board was fearing lawsuits, and legal battles that might drag on for years, depleting our already scarce funding. As suddenly as the crisis had arisen out of nowhere, we saw it settled. From time to time, when an important decision or transition was being maneuvered, he would call me in for one of our prayer times.

The last time I ever went to pray with him just before he was retiring and I was moving on. He said, "You know what I want prayer for? I want prayer that I would KNOW Jesus. I don't want to know about Jesus, I want to KNOW Jesus." I asked him what his spiritual life was like, and he mentioned that years ago as a little boy he had accepted Jesus back when he was in Sunday school. Over the years he had seen so much hypocrisy in the church, and he walked away from it all. I could feel the sourness of that memory as he spoke. At one time he had been very active in the church and been a Sunday school teacher for many years, but had been hurt and embittered by what he had seen there. What amazed me to realize in that moment was that even as he had climbed the career ladder in education, and had a very intimidating and expressive exterior, God still saw the Sunday school teacher who had spoken to children with the love of Jesus. He didn't forget this precious man, and in the last weeks before he left education and retired for good, he rededicated his life back to Jesus. As we prayed together, I thought to myself how faithful God is. When someone is really seeking like that, Jesus is going to follow up with them and pursue them in prayer until they encounter His love freshly again. I prayed, "Come, Holy Spirit," and He did.

STEALTH BOMBER
For me it's boldness when I know it's the right time. I wouldn't say anything at a superintendents' meeting or principals' meeting, I was there just to receive. If they wanted me to say something, they'd ask me to say it. During breakout sessions when it was more open to sharing, I found there would usually be someone in my group who would ask for prayer and share a difficult situation. Everything was always purposeful and low key.

We have to live with the assumption that nothing happens by coincidence. We are at a place in our lives where we are doing what we are doing because God has us there. He has a bigger plan. If you are a carrier of the Presence, then you have the authority to take charge to affect that change in any situation. You have not only the ability but also the responsibility to release His presence. I want to quote Randy Clark on this one: "If we had not been using the gift of healing before, it was out of ignorance; if we don't do it now, it's a transgression against God." Those words hit me like a brick.

My pastor once told me, "God gives us abilities; we give God availability." Those two statements have stuck with me even up to this day, and it's changed the way I operated in the workplace. When I first began my career, I would never have stepped out into situations like I do now. For me it was a process of learning to be more aware and to step out more and make myself bolder, because it didn't come naturally. I'm not naturally a bold person to go out and do stuff like this. The thing that helped me was when I internalized the realization that it wasn't about me, it's about the kingdom. It's not about my comfort and my desires. This is about God and His kingdom, and asking what is my part in this? It happened right away for me. I have heard about people having to pray 200 times or 800 times before they see their first miracle, but for me it was right away. The advice I would give to people is, "If you are thinking about it, then go for it." The whole kingdom of God can be revealed in a single moment, His purposes and destiny unlocked as we take that first step, as small or as simple as it might seem.

SUMMARY

Kairos is an ancient Greek word meaning the right, critical, or opportune moment. God is literally commissioning us to be a transforming grace to society, and we need to be open and alert to the opportune moment. If you notice in the gospels, Jesus told his disciples, "Follow me," but He never gave them any clue what would happen next. It is a process of being willing to drop our nets, and follow Him.

REFLECTION

Where am I tangled up in my fears or self-protection? What is the worst thing that could happen if I leap when I think I hear Him call? Am I willing to pay this price? The thing that helped me was when I internalized the realization that it wasn't about me, it's about the kingdom. It's not about my comfort and my desires, and again and again it is good to push past, rather, leap off these precipices.

ACTIVATION

Create a "hotlist" on a 3 x 5 index card. Walk through a typical day with Jesus by your side. He notices people; ask to hear His prodding. Write down five names to start with, but ask the Spirit to add names throughout the day. Prayer is soil preparation for the conversations and interactions that He will open up for us, as people ask us to enter, but use the "back door."

Michael D Smith

CHAPTER 8: GET OUT OF THE BOAT

Never let the odds keep you from doing what you know in your heart you were meant to do. — H. Jackson Brown, Jr.

I remember the moment when it all began for me. I was a successful professional, sitting in the back of our church listening to our pastor tell us that God is real and He wants to use us to be Jesus to the people around us. From the platform, our pastor would talk to us about God's heart and passion for the lost, that He would use anyone who was willing to reach people right in front of us who were suffering without hope. "The church is the hope of the world," he continued. "God's answer to the problems in your city is sitting in your seat." It was a darkened room, with folks from many walks of life. On Sundays I was drawn to the presence of God there, and for two years I had loved listening to stories of healing and transformation of people encountering the reality of God. It reminded me of what I experienced in Mexico, on that mission trip as a college kid. On Monday I would go back to work doing my job as usual, being a nice principal in a school with a lot of needs.

For a moment the volume turned down around me. The room was darkened with rows of people listening, sitting in soft chairs hearing the same words as me. In the front I could see my pastor speaking, but I heard the voice of the Holy Spirit directly in my heart. He told me clearly, "You think you're a risk taker, but you're a calculated risk taker. Your dad is a real risk taker." Part of me admired the courage and conviction I had always seen modeled in my dad. If he believed in something, he did it. He risked all without being afraid of things going wrong, without holding back a reserve on the side. So many times I had seen my mother clearly stand by his side in each of these decisions, regardless of the financial or social implications. Together I believe they reflected a model of courage, integrity and purpose that continued to inspire me to this day.

I wanted to be a real risk taker, fully launching myself into that childhood prayer when I had earnestly asked God to take my life and use it. In a moment, I could see that I had built many boxes around me, protecting the kind of career and lifestyle I thought I should have — that I had been blocking out the true calling of the gospel over my life. Suddenly all those teachings went from my head to my heart. I realized, "Wait a minute, I think he's talking about me. I could be doing these things." That was the realization when everything changed, and something became alive. In a moment I realized that maybe my career hadn't been about God moving me from point A to point B, just for my own benefit and a

Michael D Smith

fatter retirement, but maybe He had strategically positioned me to carry out a unique ministry with these kids and this community. I made a decision that day that my life would be truly given to God, whatever the cost.

Looking back, I can see that each of the important events in my life had been characterized by a willingness to give it all up, to follow God. As a college student, I left my fraternity, my major, and my career path when I realized that God is real and that He loves me and had a plan for my life. In my early twenties, I left it all to go down to Guatemala to serve in an orphanage and go to Bible school. As a Master's graduate, I left behind the comfortable administration jobs in Chicago to serve in the outskirts in one of the poorest, high-immigrant school districts. I had passed through the initial phases to establish myself until retirement. As an administrator, our instinct and training is not to rock the boat, but to keep things moving as smoothly as possible. Instead, I felt Jesus calling me out of the security and order of my little boat, walking into the waves of the unknown – far beyond my capacity or training – into a place that meant either failing completely, and looking like a fool, or expecting a miracle to happen.

Meanwhile, the disciples were in trouble far away from land, for a strong wind had risen, and they were fighting heavy waves. About three o'clock in the morning Jesus came toward them, walking on the water. When the disciples saw him walking on the water, they were terrified. In their fear, they cried out, "It's a ghost!" But Jesus spoke to them at once. "Don't be afraid," he said. "Take courage. I am here!"

LEAP

> *Then Peter called to him, "Lord, if it's really you, tell me to come to you, walking on the water."*
> *"Yes, come," Jesus said.*
> *So Peter went over the side of the boat and walked on the water toward Jesus.*
> Matthew 14:24-29 (NLT)

A SHIFT IN THE SPIRIT

I believe as we continue to meet with God and spend time with Him in the quiet hours of hiddenness, He downloads a different reality into our being. Peter stepping out of the boat was not a spur of the moment decision, reacting to what he was seeing, but rather the manifestation of something God had been revealing to him over time. I believe it was the outgrowth of a spiritual revelation he had that Jesus was calling us to do the same things that he did. I believe that the precious time spent with our Father reveals things to us in the Spirit about who we are and what we are called to do, long before our mind can naturally accept these realities.

I remember when I experienced this kind of shift, and it was regarding my recent transition from full-time career professional to full-time ministry. At that point in my life I would have said it was the opposite of what I wanted, but looking back I can see that my spirit seemed to know it long before my head was ready for the information. I was at a conference with my pastor and our friends Jared and Chase. We were hanging out in the green room before one of the sessions. It was a very casual time, but I suddenly noticed that something was changing in my heart. Chase asked me if I was okay, and then out of my mouth blurted the words, "I think God's calling me to be a pastor." My eyes got wide open, because it was the last thing I had in mind at this point in my life. I had my perfect job, my house in the suburbs, a nice retirement lined up for me if I would just finish it out, doing what I had studied so hard and prepared to do. In many ways, I had it "made," but something in me realized that I would be missing my destiny. I was realizing that even though I had set out to be successful and secure, in my heart I knew that the way He lived his life, full of faith and trust in God, was right. I told them, "I think I'm in the last cycle of my job."

Robby laughed. Chase said, "That's what I told you at the school." I don't remember him saying that, so I must have mentally blocked it out at the time. It was far from everything I had worked for, but at the same time I was thinking, "Wow, that must be the Holy Spirit, He must have used my lips to finally reveal to me in the physical realm what has already been revealed spiritually." It was the same kind of transition that occurred when God was calling me to move out of the natural realm at work and into the supernatural place of prayer and expectation for miracles.

When I finally realized this is what God was calling me to do, the biblical story of Peter took on a whole new meaning. Sunday school pictures show Jesus on the waves, with Peter overcoming the fears of the storm. Just him and Jesus. Now when I found Jesus calling me to make the leap, I suddenly became aware that they were not alone. They had an audience of spectators watching. The "boat" was filled with other people, people like my colleagues. With any group of humans, there is always a little competition, comparison, and criticism in play. Were they smirking when they saw Peter put his foot up to the side of the boat? These guys were seasoned fisherman, experts of storms and waters, and currents. If I imagine myself in Peter's place, my first thought could be, "If I fail, will I ever live this down?" The laughter would erupt around me as the guys watch me climb up to the side of the boat and then, with one step, drop straight into the water. Seconds later I'd be soaking wet and flailing in the waves, calling out for help, while they fish me out like a drowned rat. It takes them a few minutes though, because they are falling down with laughter, slapping each other on the backs and shouting, "Imagine, this guy thought he could actually walk on water! Who does he think he is? God?"

Sure, I believe Jesus could do miracles— even the most nominal deist will say, "Yeah, God can heal." But to believe that God could use *me* to heal? No way. I could begin to make a huge long list of reasons why He probably wouldn't do that today.

A hundred days could pass, each with the same set of excuses. Years go by. What catches my attention is this: When Jesus reaches down to lift a sinking Peter out of the water, His question is not, "How could you be so presumptuous?" Or even, "Why did you do this before you were fully ready?" His only question to Peter is, "Why did you doubt?"

Each time we made a decision for God, there were always plenty of reasons to doubt. I believe the important step is to set those aside like Peter, who is basically asking, "If this is You, Lord, call to me and I will come." He says yes to Jesus before he is even sure if it is Jesus. Not only is he willing to surrender the security of the boat, it's a picture of what a surrendered heart looks like. His security is not in his proven ability to do miraculous things, but in the fact that if it is Jesus calling to him, he will make a way. Two things are true: once you step out, God will use you and the enemy will rationalize you with fear. He'll try to tell you, "You can't do this, it's not possible." Yet when we answer His "Come," God will show the way.

SAY YES AND LET GOD DO THE REST
Seven years after making that decision, I had seen so many miracles I lost track. I had seen scores of salvations and dozens of people set free from oppressive spirits. I knew I was living out the call God had for me. One day I was working in my office, doing some busy work. It was after school hours and I was standing by my desk in my old principal's office. Tall glass windows looked out into the main office. I was standing up by my desk, stacking some large piles of papers, enjoying the quiet hum of the school which had finally emptied for the day. All of a sudden, I heard a clear knock on the wood from the bookcase behind me. I turned around and looked, and tried to see if my boss was playing a practical joke on me or something. It was a clear knock, but nobody was in sight. I peered into his office across from me, and down the hall, wondering if a stray student was waiting to be picked up. I didn't see anybody there, the rest of the staff had locked up and left half an hour ago. I thought, "That's odd, why would I hear a knock?" All of the sudden, I felt the shift in the atmosphere and I realized, "This is a holy moment."

I raised my hands in surrender and prayed, "Speak, Lord. Your servant is listening."

Immediately neon words seem to flash across my mind and become embedded there. "HELP ROBBY." Robby was my former pastor, who had moved to Texas years before to start an international ministry. In my heart I saw my old pastor and friend like a swimmer, half underwater, in a current that was strong and too fast to hold out on your own. As he swept past, I heard him cry out, "I NEED HELP!"

Suddenly it made sense to me as I realized that God had already prepared this move. This was the fifth year in the job and my contract was up for renewal. For some reason I had delayed signing, because I had a vague sense of uncertainty about the coming year. I had begun to feel uneasy about the amount of extra stuff collected in my home, and had begun giving away unused items and decluttering to get back to the essentials. That is definitely not like me, and now I knew why my Spirit had begun to respond to the shift long before I was rationally aware. I grabbed a paper and wrote out a resignation by hand.

That night I closed my car door, and thought about the news I would now share with my wife. Pack up our bags, pull our kids out of school, leave almost everything behind, and travel across the country? She was cooking in the kitchen when I set down my bags and began, "Well, you'll never guess what happened, today!" One thing about my wife is that she is an intercessor. Because she has such a special relationship with God, hardly anything surprises her.

She told me, "We are moving to Texas, aren't we." Three times in the past year we had been asked to leave Chicago, and each time we said no. We felt rooted and committed where we were. That day, God spoke to us both separately about the same thing that we had originally been opposed to. I'm so grateful that it's always been easy for my wife to recognize what God is speaking and leading, even before I do many times. While no one else around us might be able to understand what we are doing and why, it's always been a source of unity and confirmation to have Him give us both this sense of direction.

My father had a motto that always stuck with me regarding major life decisions: "When in doubt, don't." It might sound like a risk-aversion stance, but actually he was a huge risk taker who made so many sacrifices and moves in life. He made bold life decisions and was always willing to lay it on the line – yet he did this without any doubt that he was responding to a clear call from God. Throughout my life, I have applied this advice as well. Any time I have made a major change, it's come from a place where I had no doubt it came from God. Though there were many obstacles and challenges to overcome, I had no doubt in my mind that the prompting came from God.

The next day I walked into my boss' office soberly and handed my resignation to him. "Are you sure?" I had worked in District 131 for fifteen years. He took it and that was that. There were just a few weeks left in the school year. Though the future was far from certain, my heart was already resolved to say yes to God, whatever it could bring. I knew that for the rest of the transition – selling the home, moving across the country, stepping out of my ministry roles – God would provide the way. There were a lot of details to be worked out, but in each case the right people at the right time stepped forward to help us make that transition smoothly, and surprisingly quickly, as we began our new work as part of a global mission. Looking back, it seems very clear how God had been preparing the way all along, even though for almost a year I had been very resistant to any suggestion of leaving, certain that our life was in Chicago. When the time came to transition, it was actually surprisingly easy. I believe it was many small decisions I made to follow the guidance of the Holy Spirit that created such a smoothness to the process.

OUR SMALL OBEDIENCE CLEARS THE WAY FOR BIG OBEDIENCE

It would have been easy to rationally override that small still voice, in favor of what made sense from the worldly perspective. Sometimes we are excited to obey God in the "Big" decisions of life, but are quick to push away His prompting in the little ones, and let our own logic or preference override his guidance. One area where it would have been hard for me to let go was my hobbies. I've always been a tinkerer, someone who buys broken things and fixes them up. It was something I enjoyed doing, and even supported myself this way when I was younger. I've always collected projects thinking "someday I'll get to this."

One day I was lifting weights in my basement when I heard the Holy Spirit say, "You have too much stuff. It's time to get rid of the clutter." Over the rest of the year I had begun to sell and auction things off. Toward the end of the year, I realized it was time intensive and I began to more freely start giving and throwing things away. When I started getting rid of stuff, I'd start to realize that most of it was actually burdensome, bringing weight and worry to me, not value. The more stuff I got rid of, the more freedom I felt. If I didn't hear so clearly from the Holy Spirit I would have had doubts. As a collector I know the value of things, but at the same time I believe God was using it to start to set me free from that kind of value, and clearing away space to receive a bigger call from Him.

REAPING WHAT YOU SOW
I believe that as we sow in faith, we reap in faith. I have heard many sermons focusing on this from a financial perspective, but I actually believe it applies to everything we do. As we gave up ourselves generously to follow God, I saw that as we stepped out in this action of faith, we seemed to experience a similar reciprocation towards us in different areas of leadership, finances, provision, and timing. I will give a few examples.

To some, us suddenly stepping out of leadership of a school or of a church might seem irresponsible or neglecting my responsibilities. In this situation, I was able to see how it actually cleared the way to release new leaders into their ministry. There was a couple that had been volunteering over the years, serving in the children's ministry and other capacities. They were really doing great. I made an appointment to get together for lunch with the husband and I asked him, "Listen, would you guys be interested in stepping into the leadership of this church? Have you ever thought of being a pastor?"

He didn't know what to say, "What?"

I told him, "Don't even give me an answer right now. Go home and talk about it with your wife, because she has to be on board." He called me that same day because he and his wife knew that it was something he had to do, and they were honored by the invitation. I believe as radical as our response of faith was to step out of the job, there was a release of that same kind of faith to raise up the next generation of leadership.

A GOLD COIN IN A FISH BELLY

Of course, once you make a decision to follow Christ, the enemy will soon start to supply you with every imaginable excuse to delay or bow out of that obedience. When we start to hear many voices clamoring for our attention, giving us doubts and fears and anxiety and excuses, we know we must turn away because they don't come from God. Instead of many voices, we should hear one peaceful, still voice of the Holy Spirit. The busier things get, the more important it is to make a quiet time to be still and wait on his voice.

Then, rather than worry about the problems, my strategy has been to simply get busy being obedient. By the time the issue needs to be addressed, there is usually already a solution we could never have foreseen. He told us to do it and He is going to provide. Everything is there. Just do it. One small example: we had to sell our home in Illinois and we needed new carpet. I had a friend give us the name of her carpet guy. He came over the next day, measured the whole place, and gave me an estimate. He said that he could do the work the next day. He said he would leave my house, buy the carpet, and install it the next day. Even though it was a fairly low amount for the work he was doing, I asked, "Is that the best you can do?"

"Yes, but I'll give you $100 off if you can pay me cash." I went into my safe, hoping to find something. I reached into it and I pulled out an envelope of money I had never seen before and didn't remember having. When I counted the money, to the dollar it was exactly what we needed to pay for the carpet. That was at the beginning of the process of getting the house ready. It was a helpful reminder to me throughout the process. Whenever feelings of anxiety arose, I remembered that envelope and thought, "God's already got this taken care of." I just have to be faithful and remember things that He's called me to do. He has supernaturally taken care of me in the past, and He is supernaturally taking care of me now.

WORTH THE SACRIFICE
When we were clear about the call, we immediately started to obey. We flew to Texas to meet with Robby and his wife Angie, and talked about what the transition would look like, though we still did not have the answers for leaving Chicago. One game theory in basketball teaches, "the best defense is a good offense." I believe the enemy wants to keep us distracted in constant defense. But when we resist the temptation to focus on the problems and, instead, move forward toward our promises with confidence and boldness, I believe we put the enemy on the defense. God is our defender, we must continue to advance.

Many times this comes at a cost. In this case, we had to make the difficult decision to sell our house at a loss because the market was low. Financially, we lost a lot of our value in this move, yet we needed to do it in order to continue moving forward and put that money into a new home in Texas. It was a price we were willing to pay, to keep in step with what God was asking us to do. We also had to give away many items in order to fit everything into a small pod. We had two cars and I had to leave one behind. Each of these steps was a reminder to me that our treasure was not on earth, but in heaven. I also believe it was a strategic process God was putting me through, in preparation for what was ahead. Each step of the way our needs were completely provided for. When we needed money, it was there.

By the time we moved to Texas, our savings were gone. I was getting ready for the closing of our new house and needed cash. My wife reminded me that I had an open bank account still open back in Chicago with some money I had set aside for repainting the house, almost a thousand dollars. It wasn't enough for what we needed, but it would help. When I went to withdraw the money, I discovered it was $5000, exactly the amount of money we needed to cover the closing costs on our new home in Texas. So many times I have seen God provide through small, simple steps of faith. When a fisherman needed to pay the tax, Jesus had him go out and catch a fish. A fish would never have been enough to pay for the yearly tax, yet, through that small obedience, God provided exactly what was needed for that time. I don't believe we are called to wait and do nothing, but I do believe we are called to take small steps of faith and trust that God will do the rest. I am still on the journey myself of learning how this all works. I have never adhered to the "prosperity" gospel hype of "Name It and Claim It," but I do know that when we trust God and keep our focus on Him, He will equip us and provide for us to do what He is calling us to do.

We bought another home, we had insurance when we needed it, and our kids got into school without missing even a single day of class. They even made friends right away. Nothing was lost except for our money. I believe God knew that those savings had always given me a sense of security, my private back-up plan each time I took a pay cut in order to obey God by working in a lower-income district, or losing half of my salary later on in order to pastor the church. I sensed the Holy Spirit gently encouraging me that He was leading this process. "Those were things you were looking to for comfort, and I want to be Your comfort and source. I will provide."

Ever since I was a teenager, I struggled with this, especially in high school. My father is really smart and he had nearly completed a computer science degree when computers were first coming out. He was on track to become incredibly wealthy when computers took off, but instead walked away from it to follow new opportunities as he saw God leading. My parents were hippies, very generous but non-materialistic at the same time. We moved around a lot as kids. By the time I was in fifth grade, we had moved eight times. Sometimes my parents bought a house, and sometimes they rented a house. They didn't worry about money, but we didn't have a lot extra either. They trusted everything would be all right. By the time I got into high school, I realized that by giving up a career in early computer science, my father had walked away from a fortune. I imagined myself like some of my friends, with a vacation home, dirt bikes, traveling all over the world. At that time, I started to be resentful. I had a knack for making money, and started out small buying things and flipping them quickly for a profit. I was always able to make extra cash on the side, and my intention was to do the opposite of what I saw as carelessness in my dad's choices. I was on track to be a business major, and I wanted to be successful, get a good job, and make a lot of money. After twenty years of hard work to get where I was, the last thing I had in mind was to give it all up and go into ministry. I had tried that as a twenty-year-old and ended up broke and stranded, working in an orphanage in Guatemala just to get enough money to survive only to come home and start over. Then, I had nothing to lose, now I had a whole career and two degrees worth of work at stake. At the same time, the older I grew, the more I respected and admired my dad. The journey of the last fifteen years has shown me how much greater and more worthwhile God's plan is, and He always provides. When I heard God calling me to let go, once again, I leapt at the chance to obey.

WORLDLY LOSS FOR HEAVEN'S GAIN
Too many people get stressed when they try to take on things that God should be in control of. I had to face this twice. I believe many times God continues to repeat certain lessons in our life, to reveal to us both the transformation that has taken place as we react differently than we did before. Sometimes as humans, when He removes one dependency, we can simply replace it with another. Five months after settling into Texas, the coronavirus hit America and our international travel ministry was suddenly no longer international, and no longer traveling. Ten months after buying a house and owning it, we resettled again to Europe. It was yet another cost that again showed me how quickly I had begun to re-

"settle" into life, instead of releasing any dependency. I believe it's an incredible spiritual journey, when you truly decide to put your money where your mouth is, and it's one I'm living out right now.

As I make these changes, I see more spiritual fruit and opportunities opening up to me that would never have been available a year ago. As an educator, the last ten years before retirement are the most fruitful from a financial point of view. Achieving the highest level of pay possible will determine your level of retirement income and security. By giving this up, I was giving God not only everything I had been working for, but also my secure future. At the same time, I am now seeing a level of fruitfulness in ministry I never thought would be possible. God is opening doors in Europe, in formerly closed nations, to suddenly start ministering openly. What often looks like a demotion in the world's eyes, is a spiritual promotion on many levels.

Remember Peter leapt out of the boat twice: once in the midst of a great storm, but also after the death and resurrection of Jesus, when all of his plans and expectations were smashed. And Jesus met him, waiting and ready with enough.

> *Then the disciple whom Jesus loved said to Peter, "It is the Lord!" As soon as Simon Peter heard him say, "It is the Lord," he wrapped his outer garment around him (for he had taken it off) and jumped into the water. The other disciples followed in the boat, towing the net full of fish, for they were not far from shore, about a hundred yards. When they landed, they saw a fire of burning coals there with fish on it, and some bread.*
> John 21:7-9 (NIV)

Step by step, this past year has been "walking on water" with Jesus in a place of dependency, trust, and freedom. When God leads us into a season of pruning, it's painful, but the fruit it produces is unlike anything that was possible before in an unpruned vine. God is saying, "Leap."

"I can't."

"I didn't ask you if you were able, I just said to do it." When you step, all of a sudden a rock appears and you step on that rock, and another, and another. By faith you put your foot forward and God provides a place for it.

HEAVEN'S IMPOSSIBILE CALL

When God gives us an assignment, He gives us everything we need to be successful. Don't look at your bank account when God starts doing these things, because He is the Provision. Don't look at your own capacity or resources. I think automatically, "It's possible," but when God has something to do, He's going to do it despite my best efforts, and it's going to be wonderful and glorious and so much better than anything we can do. Sometimes I think that's why God keeps things so general. It is about trusting Him and not myself. If it was specific, I would probably try to make a plan and figure it out. Many times He simply says, "Come." Although His calling is impossible, He makes it possible. Jesus never rebuked Peter for getting out of the boat on a dark and stormy night. He never rebuked Peter for thinking he could walk on water. The only thing he asked him was, "Why did you doubt?" Many of us begin a journey in faith, but then become weighed down or discouraged by doubts. When you follow the clear simple voice of Jesus saying, "Come," you must keep following in the same simple, clear way, one step in front of the other.

When you're going through dark times, everything looks so hopeless, but there is usually one more thing you can do to obey God. When things look overwhelming or impossible, simply ask yourself "What is the next best step I could take to be obedient to what God called me to?" As you go about your day, before you know it, you have arrived where you needed to be and are asking yourself, "Oh my gosh! How did I do this? How did I get through this?" Just be faithful to what He's given you, and be willing to take one simple step at a time.

SUMMARY

God's heart and passion is for the lost, and He is calling each one of us to follow Him. He has spoken, "Yes, come," and we need to leap. Once you step out, God will use you. The enemy will rationalize you with fear, trying to tell you, "You can't do this, it's not possible." Yet when we answer His "Come," God will both show the way, and meet our needs, one step at a time. With Him, all things are possible.

REFLECTION

What is your boat? Is there anything in your life in which you are placing your security rather than trusting Him, and which needs to be cleared away in order to make space for His greater call?

How do you tend to deal with doubts and fears and anxieties and excuses which clamor for attention, rather than the one peaceful, still voice of the Holy Spirit?

ACTIVATION
This is an opportunity to call out to Him, *"Lord, if it's really You, tell me to come to You, walking on the water."*

Is there something He is calling you to that is getting sidetracked by fear or distraction? If it is Jesus calling to you, He will make the way.

Michael D Smith

CHAPTER 9: PRAY FOR THOSE WHO PERSECUTE YOU

Now there is a final reason I think that Jesus says, "Love your enemies." It is this: that love has within it a redemptive power. And there is a power there that eventually transforms individuals. — Martin Luther King Jr.

After my first year as a brand-new principal, my supervisor retired and I got a new boss. She was a LGBT activist, giving her life working for the marginalized and oppressed. She made it pretty clear that she saw white Christian males as the oppressive force of society, and that our district would be better served by a minority-only leadership serving a minority population in our district. I could feel the scrutiny I was up against from Day One. With some individuals, you realize immediately that their anger has nothing to do with you, but it is from a long history of triggered pain. Even though I felt somewhat misjudged, I knew that I shouldn't take things personally.

As a young believer I had been taught to always spend time with God each morning, and I believe this has been my anchor in every situation I have faced. I would wake up each morning and spend from 5-6 a.m. in prayer. One day I was really struggling. Things had been tough at work and I felt like I was getting blamed unfairly for things I had nothing to do with. In my mind, I slipped into self-pity. "You did nothing to deserve this kind of treatment. You have two Master's degrees and you speak Spanish. You can go get a job elsewhere, and you don't have to put up with any of this anymore." Each time I started to head down that path in my thoughts, I would feel God steering my heart back toward the calling He had for me, saying, "This isn't your decision to make." That particular morning when I felt like I couldn't take it anymore, as I read through my Proverbs for the day, the Lord spoke to me and said, *"The king's heart is like a stream of water directed by the LORD; he guides it wherever he pleases."* Proverbs 21:1 (NLT). In that moment I sensed the Holy Spirit speaking to my heart saying, "Our God is the one that is ultimately in control. This is the boss He gave you, and He has a reason for that. You just stick with what you're doing and don't ever argue back."

Rather than try to get God to change my circumstances and make them easier for me, I needed to simply focus on doing what He called me to do there. My purpose was to serve my staff and serve our community. From that day forward, I surrendered. I released the situation to the Lord, and confessed, "It's not about me; it's Your kingdom." Instead of praying and asking God to take away the problem or help me escape, each day I prayed and asked God to give me the strength and grace to continue to obey Him in that situation, even simply asking, "Lord help me make it through another day." I made a conscious choice to go with His plan rather than my own plan.

Each year when my contract was up for renewal, my supervisor would write negative reports about me, which I felt were unjustified, especially given my good data. It was stressful for me, but rather than defend myself, I trusted God. If He wanted to keep me in that job, nobody could get rid of me until it was time for me to go. It's what allowed me to endure, when many of my other colleagues who were facing the same pressure ended up getting discouraged and leaving. Years later when it was all over and we were both leaving the district, this boss asked me about it, mystified. "I have one more question for you, Mike. Why did you never argue back?"

"I just felt it wasn't my place, and it wasn't what I was supposed to focus on," I told her. One thing I noticed though, was that as people had brought different complaints against me, and I chose not to fight back, somehow the Holy Spirit had a way of making things happen to expose the truth in a way that suddenly made the accusations against me disappear. When we don't defend ourselves, He will. One of the lessons God has taught me in many ways is that it is important to take a strategic position instead of arguing in the flesh.

One day she had been very upset with me, and left an angry voicemail to come to her office immediately. I showed up after work, with some anxiety already building in my stomach. I poked my head in her office, and saw her sitting at her desk, rubbing her temples. I asked her, "Is everything okay?"

"Yes," she slowly replied. After a few minutes, with her back still turned to me, she admitted that actually she had just gotten back from the doctor and they had found calcification on her brain. "Would you like to pray about that?" I asked her.

She turned to look at me, staring for a moment, and slowly replied, "I'd like that."

I bowed my head, and asked "Holy Spirit Healer, come with Your loving presence."

Immediately it felt like the room tilted open wide, and a light, fresh presence of God filled the room. I prayed a prayer of command, "Brain, be healed in Jesus' name. Sickness and pain be cancelled. Holy Spirit, You are welcome here. We release peace over the office, and Your protection and presence to protect everyone in it."

It was a short prayer, only about one minute in length, but the room suddenly felt very peaceful. We sat there quietly for a couple of minutes in the presence of God. I said, "Okay, what would you like to talk about?"

She glanced down, "You know what? Never mind about that. I think I just want to go home." When I walked out the door, she said, "Hey, Mr. Smith, thank you so much for the powerful prayer."

At that point in my life we had already worked together for a few years; we knew each other. Before this, we had had a very tense relationship. This moment was a turning point in our relationship. A couple weeks went by and I didn't see her, but when I did see her again at some function, I asked, "Hey, how are the headaches?" She looked at me again, staring hard for a moment. "You know what? They are all gone." She never brought it up again. From that point on, instead of treating me with hostility as a Christian, she actually began treating me as kind of a *shaman*, or spirit guide; and a couple of times I heard her reference me to other colleagues as a healer.

She herself was very spiritual. She had told me one that every morning she would wake up and burn sage to each of the four directions. During my morning times of prayer, I began specifically praying that the Holy Spirit would show up during her quiet time and meet with her, and let her know that He was the One and He was the Truth. My rationale was that, if this was the moment in the day when she was trying to be spiritual and focused, I would pray that the Holy Spirit would meet her. I prayed for her for years.

A few years before her retirement, she came into the office to let me know she wasn't going to renew my contract. It was the same spring I had accepted an offer to begin pastoring at the local church. I also was aware that she was in a tough position, because of the tumultuous politics happening in the district, and her position was up in the air. I asked her if she would like some prayer for the transitions we were both facing, and she said, "Sure."

We prayed and I asked direction for both of us. I had a really strong feeling that within two weeks the direction would be clear. When we had finished the meeting, I told her, "Mark your calendar because God is going to reveal something to you in two weeks."

"Why did you say two weeks? That's really interesting, because that's what my spirit guide told me, that in two weeks this would all be over."

Two weeks later we met again, and everything had been resolved. God used that last meeting for real transformation and restoration in a way that I had never expected to see. As I walked back up to the steps to my office, I felt a total release of joy. It was January in Chicagoland, the wind was bitterly cold and all the colors around me were white and grey, but inside it felt like the Fourth of July.

I was moving on, she was moving on. It had been the most difficult professional relationship of my career, and yet God had had an incredible purpose in it. Why He chose me, the least likely person she wanted to receive from, I'll never know. But in that moment, I felt the lightness of realizing that all those years of stress and discouragement was worth it all. It suddenly occurred to me that she was probably the whole reason God had sent me to this district, for this time before she retired. Had I not been willing to endure the prickly parts of that dynamic, I never would have been able to reach her with a true gospel message. It brought tears to my eyes to realize how loved we are, and how relentlessly God will pursue us back into His Father's arms. As I closed the

Michael D Smith

heavy doors of my office behind me, I shook my head and laughed, "All of these nights of lost sleep, all of that anguish?"

Was for that one person.

God never told us we would not have a tough life, or that things would be easy, but He told us he would go after that one lost sheep. I think it was humbling to me because I had never really given my life and my mission in life much thought, up until that time. At that point I had done everything because it was the obvious choice, the path of least resistance: going to college, teaching, going to Guatemala. All of those things were part of this plan. If I didn't speak Spanish I would never have gotten that job in that community. I realized how selfish I had been in being so bothered by how she treated me. I was afraid of losing my job, and my pride didn't like not receiving the appreciation I believed I deserved. I had been concerned about defending my reputation, my comfort, my house mortgage, my cars, my retirement. I saw her as the obstacle, rather than the goal of all of God's love. I realized how wrong my perspective had been during those years. Jesus loved this woman with His entire life; it was no sacrifice to be part of His message of showing her this love.

After that final day with her, it felt to me like my true purpose of life was revealed to me. Of course, I had been praying for people, and trying to make the most of the opportunities God showed me, but in many ways my life had still been about me. I finally realized, "Listen, this has little to do with you, and this has everything to do with the Kingdom." When you make yourself available to be used by God, He's going to use you the way He wants to use you. If you make yourself available to be used by God, you better be genuine and you better be ready for change because He's going to take you at His word.

I knew that I was done with the job of being the principal, and God had already called me to serve the church as a pastor. I had an appointment with the superintendent, who knew my contract was not going to be renewed. When I walked into his office he was sitting at a big wooden table. He jumped up, leaned across the table and gave me a huge hug. I did not expect it and was surprised. He looked at me with huge wide eyes and almost shouted, "That is SO COOL." I LOVE IT when people lay down their life to do something for God." He was a New Age Buddhist. I had been praying with him for healing and he was starting to see some change in his eyesight. He had grown up in the Baptist church in the past, and had some hurts about church. God had started to do some transformative stuff in his life.

I told him, "Yes, I'm moving on. I'm done with education."

He said, "No, I can't do that. You are too valuable to this district. I can't let you go."

I said, "Well, I'm moving on."

"How about if I give you a part time director's job? You'll work half the hours, and you'll still make the money."

I said, "Yeah, but I would still be in charge of staff and budgets, and it's not going to end up being part time." He nodded knowingly, and offered me one more proposal.

"How about if I make you part time assistant principal, with your buddy Mark?" I loved working with Mark, and I knew we would be a great team together. With my years of experience as principal, it would be really easy for me to do a great job supporting him, but without the time-consuming responsibility for all the paperwork and meetings.

It made sense to still stay connected to the community, and keep some of the health benefits. "Well, give me a week to pray about it and I'll get back to you." My wife thought it was a very practical decision, so I took the job and started the school year, doing prayer appointments all the time, praying for healing with teachers, and seeing many of them encounter Jesus and get saved. For the next five years I continued that way, a part-time assistant principal and full-time pastor of the local church that had kickstarted me into living by the Holy Spirit.

Scripture teaches us that humans are not our enemies, but rather the powers and principalities of darkness. It's important to always resist the temptation to fight back in the physical, or you'll become used by the enemy to bring destruction to the very people that God is trying to set free. Many times in my career, I was serving under leaders that were not following protocol, or were acting deceitfully or immorally. As I continued to act according to the standard of integrity, I often felt attacked or belittled. Rather than defend myself, I felt God asking me to honor them, not to argue or defend myself. I was in submission to that authority as well, even when God was using them to bring about turnover and change.

I believe we are called to walk in complete righteousness and integrity in every area of our work and lives. When this puts us at odd with the culture around us, we are not to enter into complaining or bitterness, but continue to honor every co-worker and supervisor in our words and actions. We have to live with the assumption that nothing happens by coincidence. We are at a place in our lives where we are doing what we are doing because God has us there. He has a bigger plan. If you are a carrier of the presence, then you have the authority to take charge to affect that change in any situation. You have not only the ability but also the responsibility to release His presence. We are warned in Scripture that salty and sweet water don't flow from the same stream. It can be tempting, but don't ever be so full of your own opinion about your bosses, or your workplace, that you are not able to hear God's perspective and be open to the blessings He might want to bring through your life to the people around you.

> *And among all the parts of the body, the tongue is a flame of fire. It is a whole world of wickedness, corrupting your entire body. It can set your whole life on fire, for it is set on fire by hell itself.*
> James 3:6 (NLT)

When I'm going through discouragement and hard times, I try to keep my mouth closed. Many times the enemy will use our own mouth to destroy us. It's better to keep my mouth closed than to speak up and have to go around apologizing to people. Because of this battle, I also made a choice to never ever drink alcohol at any district or professional event. As a school principal I was constantly invited to different events with union leaders, Christmas parties, or special ceremonies. I found that these were peak times for drinking and gossip, yet I knew that if I ever released one negative word about a colleague or criticism of any of the leadership decisions, these things would eventually make their way around and years of witness would be destroyed in a second. When people feel betrayed, that stays with them for years, and even decades.

Throughout my career I would regularly seek the wisdom of God by reading the book of Proverbs. One that spoke to me early on was *"It is not for kings, O Lemuel, it is not for kings to drink wine, or for rulers to take strong drink, lest they drink and forget what has been decreed,"* Proverbs 31:4-5 (NIV). I wanted to be a godly leader and role model to my staff and the kids at my school, many of whom had never known a good role model in their life. The proverbs had many verses about controlling the tongue, and also how to deal with authorities. In the book of Ecclesiastes, the Bible tells us "Never make light of the king, even in your thoughts. And don't make fun of the powerful, even in your own bedroom. For a little bird might deliver your message and tell them what you said." Ecclesiastes 10:20 (NLT). Working in elementary and middle school, it definitely felt like there were many "winged creatures" who went around spreading matters, and I believe God shielded me from problems I would have faced if I had spoken about my frustration. We are to continually intercede for authorities over us, and see the favor and blessing of whatever place God has called us to work.

SUMMARY
Scripture teaches us that humans are not our enemies, but rather the powers and principalities of darkness. When we find ourselves in conflict, often it isn't about us, but unresolved pain or injustice. Once we carefully and humbly consider if we might be part of the problem, we can release the relationship and the felt need to defend or attack or argue in the flesh. Release the situation to the Lord, and confess, "It's not about me; it's Your kingdom." It is also important to keep your mouth closed. Again and again in Scripture we are warned that the tongue is a flame of fire.

REFLECTION
The opposite of prayer is the pitfall of gossip. Is there an area (or areas) of your life where you have been caught up in gossip or complaining? Gossip is a pebble tossed into a pond, rippling out brokenness and resentment. Commit to never gossip about anyone for any reason, at any time, rather choose to silently lift up the situation to God's loving power and grace.

ACTIVATION
Is there a relationship in your life that feels like a battlefield?
One of the lessons God has taught me in many ways is that it is important to take a strategic position instead of arguing in the flesh.
- o Ask the Lord if you have any "wicked way" or responsibility for brokenness
- o Address with confession, without any defense or rationalization

- o Add this person or group of people to your "hotlist" and faithfully release it to His purpose and kingdom.
- o Again and again, step away from pride and reaction, in silence
- o It is no sacrifice to be His love for each lost sheep

LEAP

CHAPTER 10: KNOW YOUR WHY

The world is full of suffering, and the world is also full of the overcoming of it. – Helen Keller

All of us will reach a point in life when we want to give up. The amount of energy or pain it takes to keep going forward simply does not seem worth it. The goal no longer seems viable. For some of us, it's the external circumstances that feel too crushing, too perplexing or hurtful to continue on. For others it may be a personal crisis that hits the heart, and makes our internal resolve dissolve. I remember after ten years of being married, going to school full time, and building our careers, my wife and I began to dream of building a family together. At times we had been so busy, it barely felt like we were married; we were living together doing our own thing. Both of us worked all day, took night classes, did homework on the weekends, and in between made trips to the health club. Occasionally we took vacations together. As the years slipped by and the work always kept us busy, we had to stop and ask ourselves, are we going to be career professionals or are we going to have a family? We realized that if we wanted to have kids, we would have to change our lifestyle and make space for a family. Together we began rebuilding our lives around this beautiful dream. We found a cozy home in the suburbs near my work, and sold our condo in the city. We changed our work schedules to make more time and began trying to have children. When my wife got pregnant we were thrilled. It seemed like the work and sacrifice we had put ourselves through was finally worth it. As we watched our child begin to jump and kick in the sonogram, our hearts exploded with excitement. It was truly amazing to realize that a human being had been placed in our care, was growing stronger each day, and soon would come into the world to share our life.

Then we miscarried.

A nightmare I never thought I would ever escape. Our innocent child was lifeless before we had even had a chance to speak their name, to smile into their eyes, or to hug them. How many other children had I cared for and loved as a parent, yet my own child I would never see in this world?

I remember sitting in my garage alone, on top of some kitchen cabinets I was having installed, crying. I felt broken and drained. Everything we had done was for this child and the life we would have lived together. The dream we had shared about a family had become nothing. The world seemed so harsh. I remember thinking, "Are we even doing the right thing? Maybe a family is not for us." In that period, it was hard to feel God close to me. I was doing the same things as before, but I couldn't sense Him responding in any way. I had been so confident that He was the one opening the door for me in Aurora, at that school, and finding the house between our two jobs, but how could He lead me this far and then take away the child we had waited so long to hold and care for?

I had no sense of His reassurance at that time. I didn't know if we would be able to get pregnant again; we had waited so long for the first pregnancy. My job at the new school was very, very hard. The staff I was supervising, rather than treating me with respect as a new principal, seemed to hate me and were trying everything possible to discourage me and get me to leave. I was utterly disillusioned and heartbroken. Nothing around me really seemed to make sense anymore. The house, the job, the timing, seemed all wrong. For me it felt like the collapse of a dream and, at that time, I didn't see any way forward.

I had just started going to the little church on the corner, and I remember the pastor, Robby, telling me, "You have to get right back into it. Don't let this stop you." We had no other plan at that point, so we just had to just keep going forward. Later that year, we became pregnant again with a daughter. It was during my first months working at a new school, and I was getting terrible, severe migraines. They were so bad I needed to stay home from my job. On top of that, I began having violent chest pains as well that caused my whole body to ache. I believed I was dying of a heart attack because I had all of the symptoms. I drove over to the medical clinic where they quickly wheeled me back to a room and strapped me up with electrodes. There was no doctor on call because it was the weekend, so they called the fire department to rush me in an ambulance to the hospital where I was admitted. Next to me in my hospital room was a man who was just released from prison that night. He lay in his bed talking loudly to his friends. As I lay there in pain, unable to sleep, I was miserable. I thought, "This is really the worst. I can't sleep because of pain, I hate my job, my wife is pregnant, I'm probably fighting for my life, and I have to listen to this horrible person next to me." Just then I heard him telling his buddies, "Yeah, since I didn't have anywhere else to sleep, and I was hungry, I told them I was having a heart attack, and they have to take you in, give you a room, and three meals a day."

The next day one of my principal friends came in and saw the situation. He asked the hospital if I could get another room by myself, which really encouraged me. He prayed with me, and that day they gave me an angiogram, which showed that there was nothing wrong with my heart. I simply had a virus that had caused the lining around my heart to swell and put pressure on my heart.

I was relieved and had been encouraged by my friends who helped me remember why I had come to the suburbs in the first place. I had answered a dream that God had placed in my heart. For the first time in years I was part of a church that regularly prayed for its members and had an intercessory team. They encouraged me to trust God that there was a reason I was here, even if I didn't know exactly what it was about yet. They started showing me that sometimes when we face extreme discouragement, we can take a stand of faith in the spiritual realm. Not every emotion we experience comes from us. My wife and I had been sure of the move to the suburbs, and finding this job combination had felt like a miracle. Now it seemed like nothing was going right, and at the time I wondered if I had made a big mistake. Every area of my life was looking like a dead end, and I feared being disappointed. If it wasn't for those friends and other people who prayed for me, I might have given up and gone back to my comfort zone in the city.

Throughout scripture, I have noticed a trend as the people of God step out to the calling that they have received. Many of them face situations that would tempt them to give up, just before the breakthrough happens. David had all of his family and possessions captured and taken, just before he became king. The Israelites became even more oppressed and harassed, just before they were let free. Joseph was forgotten and abandoned for two more years in prison, before the cupbearer finally mentioned him to the Pharaoh. Noah sat in the ark full of animals for a week, before any rain came. Mordecai was threatened with death by hanging, just before Esther went to the king. Each of these people faced many challenges and obstacles in their life, events which could have devastating, delays that could have made them give into hopelessness and discouragement.

Even when you know you're pointed in the right direction and you're doing what God's calling you to do, there is definitely going to be hardship. I believe there is often a time between after we answer God's call and when He begins to reveal that call, that everything about our motive, sacrifice, commitment, and purpose will be tested. When we look at someone like David in the Bible, he was anointed by God to be king over Israel, but at first he just served as a musician in the palace. Later as he was banished from the kingdom and escaping for his life, it looked like the exact opposite of what God had called him to. This pattern is repeated throughout every major figure in the Bible. The time between when the Israelites responded to the call to leave Egypt and when they finally entered the Promised Land was a long period of testing and character growth. When they finally entered the Promised Land, it was a time of constant battles which forced them to be strong and grow as a nation, dependent on God's power and intervention. In every period of hardships is an opportunity for God to mature and strengthen our character, preparing us to carry His calling. In gardening when you "stress" a plant, it causes the roots to grow deep. Winter seasons do this as well, as the old growth falls away, allowing space for new growth and fruitfulness. It is essential that we push through this time to develop perseverance and endurance. We must develop that strong base of trust at the foundation of our ministry in order for that dream to be planted and begin to grow. Faithfulness is the response which nurtures that hidden dream of God in our heart, and brings it to a place of maturity where it can manifest and come to life. In order to receive the dream, we must be willing to believe in it despite our circumstances and despite what we see in the natural.

Many times we may not even have a clear understanding yet of what that dream looks like and the bigger purpose behind it. In my early years as principal, I began to set time aside to intentionally pray in the Spirit, worship, or simply wait in God's presence. As I spent time with Him, I began to connect more and more to a sense of purpose and calling in my life. It seemed like the Scriptures I would read in my morning quiet times began to literally come true every single day. It was exciting to realize how God was speaking to me and guiding me. Around that time, I also began to turn off the radio when I drove and prayed instead, often stopping to ask God for guidance over the situations and challenges I was facing. I believe that by staying in relationship with God on a personal level as well as a missional level, God will become naturally activated in our gifts and calling. We can't do anything about the past, but in each moment we can stop and pray — "Is there more going on? Please Lord, bring more to my mind."

Sometimes those challenges come in the form of the needs of those around us. Whether it's the sickness of a family member, a challenging team environment, or an impoverished school district, rather than complaining about the burden, I believe God has often specifically allowed us to live that experience in order to manifest His kingdom and His presence there.

THE POOR WILL ALWAYS BE WITH YOU

Working in District 131, I was constantly coming into contact with people in extreme need. Whole families lived in a single room unfinished basement that was wet and cold in the winter. Babies didn't learn to walk because there wasn't enough floor space in their home. Children came to school without coats in the middle of winter, or wore the same clothes day after day because they didn't have any more. Sometimes we get so focused on our own problems and challenges, we become desensitized to the people living in our own community, and the needs happening right in front of our eyes.

We started a feeding program at our school with the organization called "Blessings in a Backpack." It's a feeding program where every kid in the school gets a backpack with enough food for each meal of the weekend, and everything could be prepared by children. The reality is that most student's parents are the working poor, working two or three jobs, and still living below the poverty level. We gave the kids backpacks, they took them home, ate the food on the weekend, and they returned them on Monday, to be filled up again with food to distribute on Friday. The grocery store would deliver food every Friday morning for parent volunteers to come in and stuff all the backpacks with food. Because I was the first one in the area to figure out the system, people from the Not-for-Profit headquarters would come in and study my model in the school.

We would get invited to fundraisers with wealthy people, with silent auctions, and even celebrities. At one of those fundraisers we were able to pray with someone who was having some difficulties, which reminded us to learn to be aware at all times, whether with the poorest person in crisis or at a major black-tie event.

A lot of times I was asked to speak at business meetings to explain why we were doing this, and the impact it was having on the community. Outside of the schools I could openly share the salvation message and explain why Jesus was the reason we were doing this. I did an infomercial with them, talking about how this impacts our communities, and Miley Cyrus was one of the major donors to this group.

A group called 100 Women in Naperville had a different cause each month, and they would give money at each of their dinner meetings. The president of the board of Blessings in a Backpack told me that I would be the perfect person to talk about this program. I put on a nice suit and prayed about what I was going to say. I talked to women about the rate of depression in the incoming immigrant groups. Blessings in a Backpack is helping their physical needs, but the reality is these people need real hope, the hope that can only come from Jesus.

People were crying as I shared many stories of hope from our schools, and about the one who is the true Giver of hope. It was a catered meal, with 100 women eating dinner. I got a chance to get up and talk and share about the need in a community, the depression, and the challenges of the working poor. People had never thought about these things, never fathomed the depth of the struggle just to survive. This was our fundraising pitch and we shared our heart with them. We ended up getting the money that night. They came over to our school with a sweepstake's check for $10,000. After that I was asked to become a speaker for Blessings in a Backpack, and help share our story at fundraising events in the community. I believe when we remember our "why," and stay true to our heavenly calling and the designer who uniquely created us, the success will follow. God was the one who put me in these positions in our community, affirming that I was doing the right thing, and that I was pointed in the right direction. It shows that God knows what He's doing, in those little changes that seem small but end up being huge decisions. There are choices we could so easily miss. I believe God is big enough that He is able to redeem any option and give us another opportunity when we make ourselves available. As we give God our availability, he gives ability.

Another area where I saw the fruit of this was in our school test rankings. Every year, school report cards are ranked against all the other schools in the state, and everybody else in the school district. Looking demographically, my elementary school had the second highest number of ELL (English language learner) students in our district, over 90%. When we got the test results and my school was in the middle, a huge improvement from years before, it showed that as educators we were succeeding, even though most of our students had just come to the States with little or no English. Each year, we had the highest mobility rate, of kids coming and going all year long because of a transient hotel within our school boundaries. We often had homeless families arriving and leaving. Education is not the first thing on their mind, with very poor studying conditions and traumatic living conditions. Despite these conditions, we were still, on average, providing the same level of results as schools that had stable, native English-speaking populations of wealthier areas in our district. We had an incredibly hard-working teaching staff, and I believe the atmosphere of peace and the sense of family and stability created in our culture of prayer was creating a turnaround in our test results. We weren't at the bottom of the list! "Amazing!" I told the teachers, "I don't know how you guys are doing this, but whatever it is, don't change a thing, because it's working!" A lot of that had to do with the culture of prayer, and we were seeing the community of faith impact clubs, tutoring programs, and a lot of extra neighborhood services that I wasn't even paying for. I believe all of us felt privileged to serve in this community, and to be able to impact the lives of students who were overcoming so many obstacles at such a young age.

LAYING IT ALL ON THE LINE

So many times in our lives we make major decisions based on money and prestige. From a very young age, I was influenced by my parents, with their hippie mentality, who would downplay decision-making based on material things. I didn't feel pressure from them to go to college or to seek a secure career. My dad's attitude was basically, "You're the one that gets out of bed for the next forty years, so you better be doing something you love to do—you have to love it." He had a different perspective than most people, putting faith first at the center of our decisions. He didn't believe that we are going to be judged for the money in our bank account, or the size of our house, but really on whether or not we did what Jesus wanted us to do.

My father's attitude was that, "If it's meant to be, it's going to work out." My parents often saw even the little things of life as being used by God for a purpose. They did not tend to panic or stress about things, because they trusted that "God is big, and He's not going to leave us stranded." Probably if my parents weren't *those kind of hippies*, I wouldn't have had that attitude about life. Many professionals can question their why and lose track of their purpose as they become increasingly stimulated by paychecks and success.

It's rather simple, but I don't think I could say it enough. If you want to stay connected to your "why," you just need to stay connected to God on a daily basis. We eat on a daily basis, we sleep on a daily basis, we shower on a daily basis – those are physical needs. Our spiritual needs are even greater and of so much more value and eternal consequence. So many people dismiss that, and even "mature" Christians lose track of the habit over the years. In that daily time in His presence, He refreshes and renews the Spirit in us. Read the Scripture, pray, wait, listen, and obey. When you follow those simple steps, miracles become commonplace. Regular quiet times give God an opportunity to keep you rooted and focused in the right direction. When you spend your time in His presence, He's going to redeem it multiple times over. Over the years, I have found that when I don't do this, my life just becomes about me. The question we have to ask is, "What is God's why?" I think about the individual students, the teachers and staff I prayed with, and the countless hearts who received God's love. His why is simple, it's all about His children, his lost sons and daughters that he gave everything to save.

Margarita was a short but very sturdy Puerto Rican middle schooler. Everybody in school knew, "You don't mess with Margarita." I'll never forget the first time I met her.

It was the spring right before we moved down to Texas. The School Board President called me and said, "There's been a shakeup here at the school district; we're going to need you to come back." A day later the Union President called me to ask if I would consider doing a short-term assignment in the district. A couple hours later the superintendent called me up, and asked me to step in for the last three months of school, at one of the middle schools where a principal vacancy unexpectedly opened up. The school was in total chaos. Policemen were on campus three times a week because of gang fights. Fights were breaking out every day on campus and mob fights were happening once a month. With the timing of our move being still a few months away, I accepted the position and came back to finish the school year.

I walked into the cafeteria just in time to see Margarita lunge over the top of the lunch table, grab a girl by the back of the neck, and slam her against the wall, sending a lunch lady hurling to the ground, knocking down five or six other kids. She began beating two of the girls and nobody could get her off them until two monitors came in to restrain her. Later, when she had calmed down in my office, Margarita was horrified to find out she had hurt the lunch lady. "Oh, I hurt Ms. Chavez?" She buried her face in her hands and seemed close to tears. She was one of her favorite lunch monitors, and Margarita knew her temper was out of control. My heart went out to this girl. She was still just a kid. How much violence had she witnessed in her short little life to make her act this way and fill her with so much rage? She was often in my office, sent out of the classroom for mouthing off, disrupting classes, or threatening other students. Margarita came from desperate poverty. She owned nothing, and I noticed over the school year that she literally wore the same clothes every day to school. She had a girlfriend, and for some reason she liked me, but other than that, she didn't have many friends at school. The other students and teachers in the school were all terrified of her. She told people she thought I was "peaceful." Nobody else in the school could get her to stop fighting when she was in a rage, but when I would walk up and call her name, and touch her shoulder, she would immediately stop fighting and apologize.

One of the things I knew about her was that she loved sunflowers. Toward the end of the school year, I wanted to give her something that she would like. I found a wall ornament of sunflowers, with a quote on it about hope and choosing your path in life. On the last day of school, I told her, "If you can make it through this last day of school without fighting, I'll give you a present." She was so happy and made it all the way through the end of the school day without fighting. I had even seen her walk away from several kids who were provoking her, a situation I knew she would usually never let pass. When the dismissal bell rang, she marched into my office and stood in the doorway, "Well, sir!?" she said, "Where's my stuff? I didn't fight nobody today." I gave her the sunflower plaque and the note I had written about why she was like a sunflower, and had so much sunshine to fill this world. She was the "worst" kid in the school, always involved in screaming fights and violence, yet in a moment, her soft brown eyes filled with tears and she beamed with a smile that lit up her whole face. "Thank you so much, sir, I'll never forget you." She hugged me and ran out the door.

Here was God's daughter. He loves her with all of His heart, and He knows every single thing that she has endured since her birth. As the buses pulled up, she tapped on the window and held up her sunflower plaque, hugging it and waving to me. I never saw her again after that day, but I knew that for the first time in school, maybe in her life, she had felt loved and seen. God's "why" are His kids, and when we spend time with Him, He will help us recognize them in all of the disguises life has made them wear.

As we headed to Texas to work with a global team, and then on to Europe, I remain forever grateful for the lessons I learned in East Aurora. It was a place that showed me the depths of God's love for humanity. In all of our weakness, sickness, pain, and problems, His presence is always there, waiting to be invited into any moment, any situation. His love is able to overcome the hardest heart, and restore relationships, families, and community. As we live our days in His light, following in the prompting of the Holy Spirit, we get the joy and privilege to carry the ministry of Jesus: binding up the brokenhearted, bringing release from darkness for the prisoners, giving a garment of praise where there had been a spirit of despair. We have the privilege to announce the good news that this is the year of God's favor, a time for salvation that is open to each one of us. It's a message that is far more beautiful and breathtaking than most of us have ever imagined.

SUMMARY
As we journey in obedience and faith to the dreams God has put in our heart, we will face obstacles, setbacks and pain that will tempt us to doubt God, to give up, or look for an easier way out. Sometimes faith looks like stepping out boldly in the direction God has called us and risking it all despite circumstances or obstacles. Other times it looks like surrendering in trust that God will provide the way, and continuing to live out our daily life in obedience and connection.

REFLECTION
Is there an area of your life where you have lost a sense of hope or excitement? Many times discouragement and unbelief can enter our life through disappointment or pain. Sometimes our own

failings can lead us to a sense of disqualification, questioning whether or not God would still use us. Think through the major dreams of your life, whether it's marriage, career, ministry, family, the kind of person who you hoped to become. How easy is it for you to believe that God is at work in this area of your life and has a good plan for you?

ACTIVATION
This activity is a listening prayer exercise. If there is an area of your life that doesn't glisten with hope, it could be that you have become discouraged or have believed a lie in this area of your life.
- Ask the Holy Spirit to help you jot down any areas where your hope is not strong.
- Pray and ask Jesus to show you at what point did this hopelessness enter in.
- As you become aware of that time in your life, ask Jesus if there is anyone you need to forgive in that moment (including yourself).
- Next, ask the Holy Spirit to show you if there is a lie you believed in that moment.
- Ask Jesus to show you instead, what is the truth about the situation, or about you.
- Ask the Holy Spirit if there is any way he wants to encourage you in this area of your life.
- Finally, read through two Psalms, and ask the Holy Spirit to speak to you through his word, and confirm what he is saying.

Repeat these steps for any other feelings of anxiety, fear, or discouragement that you may be facing in your journey. Many times I have seen God use these kinds of prayer encounters to minister truth, encouragement, and breakthrough in areas of our life where we may be discouraged. Continue to read over any encouraging words you receive. Jesus promised to send us His Comforter, because He knew we would face many challenges and difficulties in this life.

Michael D Smith

AFTERWORD

Throughout my life, I've often reflected back on the legacy of my father, and now on my own legacy that I am passing to my own kids. I've come so much to appreciate the trust in God and total abandon with which my dad lived his life. As my own faith in God grew, I began to realize how powerful and important it is for us to give ourselves permission to really take risks, and to live in freedom that comes from knowing that God is so big, and truly able to take care of us. As we step into this reality, we experience the truth that all things are possible *to him that believes*.

Sometimes the process is messier than we can imagine, and full of surprises. In 2019, I left the security of my job and retirement, sold my home, left all my friends and connections behind, and moved down to Texas to support a global ministry of miracles and evangelism in the Muslim world. When COVID hit, suddenly everything came to a standstill, and my job overseeing international travel itineraries and conferences no longer existed. It might have seemed like a total loss, except that God had other plans. With our kids now in online schooling, my wife and I were able to accept an invitation to move to Poland to help with a business startup, as well as do some ministry. Once again, we sold our home, less than a year after purchasing, gave our dog to a friend, and moved to Poland.

Suddenly my years of experience working in a mostly Catholic neighborhood came into use. A Catholic Charismatic community here invited me to begin speaking and ministering in what is a growing revival among Polish Catholics. My wife and I became the first evangelicals ever to be allowed to do so, because of the massive rift between the churches here. On a regular basis, I am seeing people healed, giving their lives to Christ, and weeping under the touch of God's presence. We also assist in a Charismatic Catholic homegroup and a local Pentecostal church.

Our business startup is taking off with an explosion, even in the midst of the COVID economic crisis. Before leaving America, we received a prophetic word from a well-known prophet who knew nothing about us or what we were doing. He told us that we were going to restart a business, and we will get the bids because we are known as honest people, even though we are not the cheapest bid. He told us we would be working in a corrupt environment, with corrupt people, but we would be trusted. The reason the Polish leader invited me was because his former business partner had robbed him of everything he owned, and he had not been able to find anyone he could trust to work with. Corruption and graft are common in this post-soviet economy, but we have seen our business model and honest practices open doors with the most unlikely people.

As we pray for healing, it's the first time I am seeing this level of depth in the emotional and spiritual healing that God is doing. Because of the virus, we have also been able to open up online prayer appointments with hundreds of people who would never usually have stepped foot inside a church. We have seen God divinely orchestrating each detail, from the housing and vehicle that were provided when we arrived here, to the incredible divine appointments he set up for us.

Michael D Smith

Soon after we arrived in Poland, the pastor of the church introduced a man who was going to give the message instead of him, a man who had been a missionary for many years and was likely going through a discouraging time. As the pastor prayed for him, he asked that God show him some of the fruit of his early ministry, to encourage him, and to show him how valuable his life had been. When the man stood up to speak, I realized it was the Polish missionary working in Chicago that had taken me under his wing as a college student where I got saved. I walked up to him afterwards and said "Wiesiek Stebnicki." He hadn't seen me in 30 years and had no idea who I was. As I shared with him the impact of that trip on my life, suddenly his eyes widened in disbelief. I was able to share with him how much God had used that time to change my life, set me on a life path of ministry, and even bring me back to Poland now to serve in the churches, and to continue to see what God has in store for us. Each step taken in faith can have an eternal ripple of impact on the lives of others.

Years before, our entire path toward Poland was actually because of a Polish couple named Darek and Agnieszka Jaduszyńscy. They were born-again believers in the Catholic church wanting to see God move and awaken Poland. They had reached out to Robby asking for prayer more than a decade ago. It was an unusual connection, because they had seen a message by my pastor and felt the Lord wanted to connect them to him, even though he specifically said in the video that he did not respond to message requests for prayer, everything was already available in Christ according to scripture. Darek wanted to reach out to him anyway and finally they wrote to him asking for prayer, and prayed that he would respond in three days. Robby did respond on the third day and told them that my wife, Bogusia, was going to follow up with them. Robby then asked us to follow up as the message sent to him was supernaturally highlighted. He receives hundreds of messages each week and this one was different than the rest. That is how Bogusia and I met Darek and Agnieska, and our fellowship over the years continued. In 2020, in the midst of the coronavirus pandemic, they asked us to join their work in Poland, gave us a company car and found us cheap housing. They are probably the most generous people I have ever met. They not only look out for us, but many others as well. They were part of helping us understand a dream my wife received, and I believe they will be a significant part of the revival to come.

Several years before, my wife had a dream of a map. She was standing on a train platform and a train came in. It wasn't leaving yet, but it stopped. There was someone looking at her, she didn't know him. All of a sudden the train tracks disappeared and went under water. She looked at the man and asked him, "Did you see that?" He told her, "You were not crazy, that just happened." The vision of the map was so vivid she drew a picture of the map when she woke up. We reached out to some prophetic people during that time who shared with us the interpretation they believed the dream meant – a coming revival. Later we were on a conference call with her cousins in Poland who were starting a homegroup. We met with them regularly online to pray with them about their work in Poland, and about what God was speaking. My wife wanted to share with them about the dream in case it meant something to them. Just before the call, the Holy Spirit spoke the word "SOBIBOR" to me. We were sharing with them about the dream, and I kept hearing, "SOBIBOR." I had no clue what that meant. We googled it, and it was a location in Poland where one of Hitler's death camps was located. It was a strategic location where Belarus, Poland, and Ukraine all met together, across from a river. My wife held up the paper where she had drawn a picture of the map in her dream. It was different from the modern day. When we found an older map of the original station and river during WWII, it lined up perfectly. The original train platform that Hitler built is still used there today, it's all that remains as he destroyed the rest of the camp to try to hide evidence. It was a camp that had revolted from Nazi control, and successfully fought for freedom. We believe there is a spirit of breakthrough and revival that will breakout from this place.

In Proverbs, it's written that some things are hidden and it's up to a king to search them out. I needed a prophet, someone who could pray about this dream. We reached out to Phil Urena, we gave him the dream, and his prophetic team interpreted it. This is a prophetic dream telling us about a coming revival. The blood of the martyrs is crying out for revenge. My wife and I have begun praying over the valley of dry bones, that God would raise up a new army that would bring life and restoration all over Poland. This happened years before, and now the communities we have partnered with there are helping people by offering hospitality, thinking of others, taking care of families, and taking care of their own home groups, which they call communities – even though all of this comes at a steep cost to themselves. They are seeking revival in Poland.

We serve a God that is real, that cares for us, and that calls us to an adventure far greater than anything we could have imagined. He wastes nothing, and each of the details of our life are accounted for. As we give ourselves to serve Him, He will use each of the parts of who we are for a kingdom purpose greater than we could ever imagine. Keep taking risks, keep believing God. Don't shrink back, because He is powerful and mighty and able to do far more than we could possibly imagine.

www.ingramcontent.com/pod-product-compliance
Lightning Source LLC
Chambersburg PA
CBHW072051110526
44590CB00018B/3125